NEW PATHS

*This seventh publication in the series
"Collected Writings of the Orpheus Institute"
is edited by Darla Crispin*

NEW PATHS

Aspects of Music Theory and Aesthetics in the Age of Romanticism

John Neubauer

Janet Schmalfeldt

Scott Burnham

Susan Youens

Jim Samson

COLLECTED WRITINGS OF THE

ORPHEUS

INSTITUTE

Leuven University Press

2009

CONTENTS

FRESH TRACKS, RETRACINGS
AND DIVERIONS

The title *New Paths* will always be associated with Robert Schumann's coinage of the phrase — "Neue Bahnen" — as the title of his article in the *Neue Zeitschrift für Musik* for October 1853which encapsulated his view of the way forward for German music. This important piece is now remembered for its near-prophetic statement that an as-yet unpublished composer, Johannes Brahms, would compose a body of musical works that would come to embody an ideal of musical expression perfectly fitting for its times. Perhaps less presciently, given the benefit of hindsight, Schumann also listed in a footnote other "significant talents", namely Joseph Joachim, Ernst Naumann, Ludwig Normann, Woldemar Bangiel, Theodore Kirchner, Julius Schaeffer "not to forget that profound aspirant to great art C. F. Wilsing". Niels Gade, C. F. Mangold, Robert Franz and Stephen Heller are also credited as "bravely advancing heralds".

Schumann's key purpose in this article was to counterpoise his vision of the future to that of the then editor of the *Neue Zeitschrift*, Franz Brendel. Brendel was a strong advocate of the New German School gathered around Franz Liszt in Weimar. In November 1852, he had published an article of his own suggesting that a "rosy dawn of the future" was detectable in Weimar whereas elsewhere was to be found only "our epoch in its death throes".[1] As the founder of the *Neue Zeitschrift*, Schumann clearly felt the need to rebalance the pro-Lisztian bias of its current editor, but it is far from uncharacteristic of history that it is the response we now remember, not the stimulus that provoked it. With this in mind, it is apt that the five intriguing and unusual articles grouped here under the title **New Paths** each invite us to re-enter the ostensibly familiar territory of nineteenth-century scholarship in a fresh and re-contextualising manner. They do this variously: by retracing the historical contexts within which key musical terms evolved; by illuminating novel

---

1. Franz Brendel, "Ein dritter Ausflug nach Weimar", *Neue Zeitschrift für Musik*, (1852), p. 225.

aspects of well-known compositions; by uncovering little-known materials pertaining to composers of the canon; or by re-appraising largely obscure musical figures who merit deeper consideration.

Schumann's critical writing formed in total a kind of idealistic artistic manifesto, one in which art was viewed as a means for human betterment, and one in critical writing itself should form part of this great enterprise of progress. Little wonder, then, that music theory and musicology have frequently taken up the term "New Paths" when reflecting back upon Schumann's own compositional and critical life projects. In this collection, however, Schumann is an *éminence grise* whose influence is implicit rather than explicit. The volume does not directly address Schumann, but is a compilation of post-millennial musings on a broader range of issues concerning critical theory as it pertains to nineteenth-century Western music. It revisits some of the figures of the canon — Beethoven, Schubert and Chopin, but does so via criticism which is informed by contemporary concerns, especially those of musical practice. The "New Paths" traced by the various articles are signposted in a corresponding variety of ways, reflecting the volume's broad interdisciplinary approach. This is an approach which lies at the heart of the work of the Orpheus Institute and informs its full range of activities — postgraduate education programmes, seminars and research.

Every year, the Orpheus Institute holds its International Orpheus Academy for Music & Theory. In 2005, the Academy, brought together music theoreticians and analysts to share some of their current preoccupations about nineteenth century music within a research environment that focused specifically upon questions concerning musical creation, as part of the wider discourse on "research in-and-through musical practice". **New Paths** collates and records the contributions of the principal speakers at the 2005 Academy: John Neubauer (University of Amsterdam), Janet Schmalfeldt (Tufts University), Scott Burnham (Princeton University), Susan Youens (University of Notre Dame) and Jim Samson (Royal Holloway, University of London). Reflecting the nature of this gathering of individuals, **New Paths** does not display a uniformly "traditional" approach to music analysis, but offers a series of insights that can challenge and surprise us.

John Neubauer's comprehensive text, "Organicism and Music Theory" forms an ideal opening to the collection. Organicism is a key trope in the discussion of nineteenth century music; indeed, as Neubauer points out, the term remains relevant to us, long past an age in which it was in seemingly perfect alignment with the musical Zeitgeist. Neubauer provides a searching review of the literature on organicism, from the writings of antiquity to the present day. In doing so, he reminds us of just how central debates upon the subject have been in music theory, and how important an evolving definition remains, even in the post-modern age.

In the first of two articles on Ludwig van Beethoven, Janet Schmalfeldt examines the musical evolution of the *Sonata for Violin and Piano Op. 47*—the so-called "Kreutzer Sonata"— through the work of one of Beethoven's collaborators, the renowned virtuoso violinist, George Augustus Polgreen Bridgetower. In her article, "Beethoven's 'Bridgetower' Sonata, Op. 47", as well as providing Bridgetower with the recognition that would seem to be his due, she provides specific insights into how the relationship between violinist and pianist/composer was catalytic in the genesis of the work, and in doing so, raises more general points about the nature of collaborations between composers and performers, especially when the composer is also a performing partner.

In "Intimacy and Impersonality in Late Beethoven: Contrast and the Staging of Subjectivity" Scott Burnham presents a challenge to aficionados of Beethoven's late works, by considering afresh how these compositions embody the juxtaposition of the monumental and the personal. By doing so, he asserts that we will find new ways to read these works, and that these may go beyond the more generally accepted view of the late works as articulating an aesthetic of fragmentation.

Susan Youens interprets the "New Paths" theme as an invitation to shine a light upon a little-known musical figure. She makes a series of compelling arguments in support of her view that certain of the songs of Franz Lachner may stand alongside those of Franz Schubert as worthy examples of the "early nineteenth-century architects of sound who sought to extend the limits of the *Lied*".

Finally, Jim Samson's intriguing study of the many influences imparted to the young Frédéric Chopin through his teacher Józef

Elsner, reminds us that musical genius does not evolve in an idealistic vacuum. On the contrary, he suggests that the pedagogical stamp of Elsner can be detected throughout Chopin's oeuvre. Schumann's famous declaration within the December 1831 *Neue Zeitschrift für Musik*, in reviewing Chopin's *Variations on "La ci darem la mano"*, Op. 2, "Hats off, gentlemen! A genius" is one example of many kinds of apocrypha that have made it more difficult to understand Chopin as having a complex dependency upon his social world. Samson's article provides us with rich details about Chopin's environment, helping us to appreciate afresh the breadth of his accomplishments.

It was essentially the nineteenth century that bequeathed to us the notions of novelty, progress and the ever-present artistic calling to follow "New Paths". However, as was seen at the outset, nineteenth-century views on what constituted the new were by no means unanimous, nor without polemical wrangling. The articles ary view that newness is polyvalent and, if sought after with sufficient care and discrimination, is to be found in reappraisal of the familiar as much as in striking forth into uncharted territory. It is in this spirit that these **New Paths** are offered to the reader.

June 2009
Darla M. Crispin
Orpheus Research Centre in Music, Ghent

ORGANICISM AND MUSIC THEORY

John Neubauer

1.

GENERAL FEATURES OF ORGANICISM

"None of the arts has been affected more deeply than music by the ideology of organicism; its baleful influence is still very much with us"—writes Joseph Kerman in his introductory volume on *Musicology* (65); Christopher Norris remarks that the "powerful ideology" of organic form "acquired a central—well-nigh unquestioned—prominence in the thinking of 19th-century composers, critics and music theorists" (110).

What do Kerman and Norris mean by "organicism", this awkward term, and why do they condemn its effects so vehemently? I shall offer some answers, but the task will be difficult for, like all such terms, organicism has accrued a cluster of meanings through history, and these change their hues according to time, place, and perspective.

In the widest sense, organicism is an interpretive metaphor that imposes some aspect of organic life on objects perceived. The standard, though simplified, approach to organicism is to set it up as a Romantic metaphor against the Enlightenment's mechanistic worldview. Enlightenment thought derives, in this sense, from Newtonian physics, a mechanistic worldview in which physical processes (including light) are visualized as collisions between solid particles that exchange impulses. By the end of the eighteenth century, this world view ran into theoretical and practical problems, as did the related cosmology of a mechanical clockwork winding down. Attention shifted from physical mechanics to physiology and biology—just as would happen in the second half of the twentieth century. The shift is well exemplified by the following passage from Samuel Taylor Coleridge's *1812–13 Lectures on Belles Lettres*, which contrasts externally-imposed forms with forms that develop organically out of an inner principle. Specifically organicist is the view that, as Coleridge writes, Shakespeare is "nature humanized":

The form is mechanic when on any given material we impress a predetermined form, not necessarily arising out of the properties of the material—as when to a mass of wet clay we give whatever shape we wish it to
retain when hardened—The organic form on the other hand is innate,
it shapes as it develops itself from within, and the fullness of its development is one & the same with the perfection of its outward Form.
Such is the Life, such the form—Nature, the prime Genial Artist, [...]
even such is the appropriate Excellence of her chosen Poet, of our own
Shakespeare himself a Nature humanized (5.1: 495).[1]

A variant of this may be found in A.B. Marx's *Die Lehre von der
musikalischen Komposition*:

[the theory of composition] is not a rough dead *mechanism* that only
constitutes machines, but a live *organism* that acquires life and stimu-
lates living work, living development.[2]

2.

BIRTH AND GROWTH OF ORGANICISM:
A CRITICAL LOOK AT THE LITERATURE

Western conceptions of organicism go back to Antiquity. G.N.G.
Orsini's entry on "Organicism" in the *Dictionary of the History
of Ideas* discusses the concept in Aristotle, Plato, and Plotinus
(421–24). Caroline van Eck's more recent study of *Organicism in
Nineteenth-Century Architecture* traces the concept to alternative
sources, namely to Classical rhetoric, especially to Cicero's notion
of *concinnitas* and to Vitruvius. From there, she traces the concept
to the Renaissance, in particular to Alberti.

---

1. Coleridge actually adopted, some say plagiarized, this passage from August
Wilhelm Schlegel's 1811 lectures on European drama—but this is irrelevant for my
present purposes. Later I shall discuss August Wilhelm Schlegel in his own right.
2. [die Kompositionslehre] "ist nicht ein todter schroffer *Mechanismus,* der nur
Maschinen bildet, sondern ein lebendiger *Organismus,* der Leben sich angewinnt und
lebendiges Werken, lebendige Entwicklung hervorlockt" (Anhang, Vorwort 465).

Although it is possible to find organicism in several sixteenth- and seventeenth-century authors (Orsini mentions Heinsius, Boileau, and Pope), scholars generally agree that modern conceptions of it emerged in the later eighteenth century. They usually neglect, thereby, developments in earlier eighteenth-century science, which gave rise to a cluster of ideas that the Romantic generation then used in formulating the organicist credo.

Eighteenth-century science had two narrative accounts for the propagation of species. In the theory of *preformation* (*Einschachte-lung* or *emboîtment*) all descendants were considered to be present as miniatures of the oldest ancestor or originator. Around the end of the eighteenth century, preformation was replaced by the theory of *epigenesis*, which claimed that the developmental force was not predetermined but rather innate to each organic being. Although important physiologists like Lazzaro Spallanzani and Albrecht von Haller opposed the new theory on account of its materialist potential, physiologists and philosophers of the next generation continued to elaborate the notion that organic beings possessed some innate force. Charles Bonnet distinguished between two versions, and he labelled them with terms that have recently been revived by the humanities: one could believe either that the seeds were everywhere (*dissémination*) or that they descended from Adam and Eve (*mise-en-abîme*); Georges-Louis Buffon developed the idea of a *moule intérieure*, Caspar Friedrich Wolff that of a *vis essentialis*, Friedrich Blumenbach the *Bildungstrieb*, and Johann Gottfried von Herder, building on Blumenbach, a theory of multiple life forces (see Müller-Sievers).

Epigenesis became important for Romantic poets and idealist philosophers. As I have shown in my article "Epigenetische Literaturgeschichten", August Wilhelm Schlegel delineated this new, epigenetic concept of literary history in his 1811 lectures on European drama. In one of the famous passages, Schlegel turns against Johann Joachim Winckelmann's doctrine that the modern arts must imitate the Classical ones. In Schlegel's view, Shakespeare and Calderón are a match for the ancients, even if they do not follow theatrical rules derived from them. Instead of mechanically imposing ancient forms on their material, they adopted forms that developed from their own material and age. It is this "inner-determined" form that Schlegel regards as organic. Seen this way, organic form manifests autonomy and self-organization. Translating the epigenetic, biological principle into a principle of theatre history, this means that each age must develop, "from the inside" so to speak, its proper theatrical forms:

> ...the spirit of poetry is eternal but it passes through different bodies, as it were, and each time it becomes incarnate in humanity it has to bring about a new body, must build for itself a differently constructed body from the nourishments of a changed epoch. Forms change with the direction of poetic sensibility; to label new poetic forms as old genres and to judge them in terms of them is to make an utterly inadmissible use of the reputation that classical antiquity enjoys. Nobody should be judged by a court that has no jurisdiction over him. We gladly admit that most dramatic works of the English and Spanish poets are neither tragedies nor comedies in the ancient sense; they are romantic theater.[3]

Though the passage does not specifically mention epigenesis, Schlegel's biological simile hinges on the epigenetic view that each organism develops from an inner principle, and not from a pre-existent one adopted from the ancestors, as the preformationists had held until the last decades of the eighteenth century. As Schlegel argues, it is unfair to judge English and Spanish theatre in terms of criteria derived from ancient tragedies and comedies; the spirit of poetry impregnates each epoch differently, so that new artforms come about. The imagery may seem Romantic and fanciful, but it relies on biological discourse: literature perpetuates itself by means of epigeneses (repeated new generations) rather than mechanical preformation. By implication, both genres and national literary cultures are free to determine themselves, and are not predetermined

---

3. [Hieraus leuchtet ein, daß] der unvergängliche, aber gleichsam durch verschiedne Körper wandernde Geist der Poesie, so oft er sich im Menschengeschlechte neu gebiert, aus den Nahrungsstoffen eines veränderten Zeitalters sich auch einen anders gestalteten Leib zubilden muß. Mit der Richtung des dichterischen Sinnes wechseln die Formen, und wenn man die neuen Dichtarten mit den alten Gattungsnamen belegt, und sie nach deren Begriffe beurtheilt, so ist dieß eine ganz unbefugte Anwendung von dem Ansehen des classischen Alterthums. Niemand soll vor einer Gerichtsbarkeit belangt werden, unter die er nicht gehört. Wir können gern zugeben, die meisten dramatischen Werke der englischen und spanischen Dichter seyen im Sinne der Alten weder Tragödien noch Komödien: es sind eben romantische Schauspiele. (*Vorlesungen über dramatische Kunst und Literatur* 2: 112)

by the canonized forms of tradition. The biological metaphor is not restrictive but liberating, allowing free movement throughout the centuries and across national boundaries.

One of the best known and widest-ranging studies of modern organicism, M.H. Abram's *The Mirror and the Lamp* (1953), ignores these and other biological issues and starts, instead, with humanists like Herder (Abrams 204–205). Abrams distinguishes between three major dimensions in organicism: organic history, organic evaluation, and organic law (218, 220, 222). I shall deal with organic conceptions of history later. Under "organic evaluation" Abrams brings together rather diffuse aspects, the most important of which are the glorification of the open-ended and imperfect, and using as a criterion of aesthetic judgment the reconciliation of discordant qualities or unification of multiplicity. "Organic law," finally, means for Abrams that artworks are not fundamentally different from products of nature and therefore follow similar laws.

Samuel Taylor Coleridge is, of course, Abrams's key figure. Coleridge's nature, writes Abrams, is basically biological, and this biological nature offers him a model according to which poetic creativity is a self-organizing activity that assimilates disparate materials into an integral whole (Abrams 124). Abrams identifies four aspects of a plant as key to Coleridge's organicism: 1) it originates in a seed, 2) it grows, 3) it assimilates to its own substance the alien and diverse elements of earth, air, light, and water, and 4) it evolves spontaneously from an internal source of energy and organizes itself into its proper form (Abrams 171–72).

But is Coleridge's critical writing really "a jungle of vegetation" (Abrams 169)? *The Mirror and the Lamp*, which appeared in 1953, had to rely on incomplete editions of Coleridge's works. Even a cursory glance at the indices of the new collected works of Coleridge in the Bollingen Series shows, however, that "organism" and its cognates occur quite seldom in Coleridge's texts. The index of the *Biographia Literaria* shows, for instance, that "organic" and "organicism" do not occur in this key text of Coleridge: all entries in the index refer the reader to the introduction or to other texts by Coleridge.

The case of Johann Wolfgang von Goethe, the second key figure in studies of organicism, is even more complicated. Both in my contributions to the Munich Goethe Edition (*Münchner Goethe-Ausgabe*) and in various articles, I have tried to combat what, in my view, are misunderstandings of Goethe's morphology and of his view on the relationship between nature and art. That natural and artistic processes were analogous, if not identical, for Goethe is often asserted.[4] Yet, in key texts, such as his commentaries on Diderot's *Essay sur la peinture*, Goethe repeatedly argued against naturalistic views of the arts, and he warned against confusing nature and art. Organic beings can change their form, whereas inorganic ones, including works of art, cannot. As for morphology, Caroline van Eck (e.g. 106, 216, and 218) and many others attribute all too much weight to Goethe's notion of the *Urpflanze* (archetypal plant), which Goethe entertained only in scattered travel notes during his Italian journey and subsequently abandoned completely. He does not mention it in his *Metamorphosis of Plants* (1790), his most important contribution to botany, nor does it play any role in the theory of morphology that he developed in the 1790s, with special attention to the animal kingdom. Morphology, for Goethe, meant that all existing "inorganic, vegetative, animal, and human" beings must appear and show themselves. The essence of biological form, of *Gestalt*, is that it evolves and then perishes. The study of such biological forms is *Gestaltenlehre*, a morphological study that deals with the metamorphoses of inorganic as well as organic form.[5] Morphology may therefore be called a method rather than a subject matter (*Sämtliche Werke* 4.2:200), a visual and imaginative study of unceasingly transforming shapes (*Sämtliche Werke* 12:13).

Two aspects characterize Goethe's ideas on organic metamorphosis and morphology. First, metamorphosis (as in the case of the plant in *Die Metamorphose der Pflanzen*) does not encompass evolution; it merely interrelates homologous parts *within* a particular living form. Goethe follows the life of a plant from the cotyledons through the leaves, sepals, petals, pistils, stamen, and fruits. All these parts represent variations on a basic form. One plant does not metamorphose

---

4. "This view of artistic invention as a process of nature within the realm of mind becomes a cardinal theme in the aesthetic theory of Goethe's mature years" (Abrams 206).
5. *Morphologie* (*Sämtliche Werke* 4.2:188). See also *Allgemeines Schema zur ganzen Abhandlung der Morphologie* (*Sämtliche Werke* 4.2:196), *Betrachtung über Morphologie* (*Sämtliche Werke* 4.2:197–200), *Betrachtung über Morphologie überhaupt* (*Sämtliche Werke* 4.2:200–204) and Goethe's letter to Schiller, November 12, 1796.

into another; the species are fixed forever. The second, fuller type of organic narrative came about only with Darwin's evolutionary theory, but this, as we know, speaks of natural selection, not of metamorphoses. As Abrams rightly remarks (173), Goethe, unlike Coleridge, consistently rejected all forms of teleology. Natural entities have only an internal purpose (*Selbstzweck*), and no purpose beyond themselves. It is here, as Orsini and others note, that Goethe's notion of natural beings comes close to Kant's concept of artworks, which are, according to him, purposive but without any particular purpose (*Zweckmässigkeit ohne Zweck*). The second aspect of Goethe's ideas is that mutations within a species follow an internal principle of economy, which assures that change in one part is compensated by an inverse change in another one (*Sämtliche Werke* 3.2:313 and 12:154 f).

Goethe's notes on these principles of metamorphosis and morphology were written in the 1790s, but they were not published until around 1820. Moreover, they became widely-known only a decade later, above all in connection with the so-called Académie-debate between the French biologists, George Cuvier and Geoffroy Saint Hilaire, in which Goethe still participated (see Appel). Geoffroy, whose *unité de composition* held that different bones were morphologically homologous (analogous) to each other, regarded Goethe as a kindred soul, but Goethe had also ties with Cuvier and reservations about Geoffroy's theory. The debate had its impact on the French intellectuals, writers, and—as van Eck has shown (220 ff)—on architects, but whether it had a similar effect in German culture is a somewhat moot point. Indeed, evidence is insufficient to prove that the organicist ideas which van Eck attributes to Karl Friedrich Schinkel (146–62), Carl Gottlieb Wilhelm Bötticher (163–74), and Gottfried Semper (228–34) are indebted to Goethe.

Similar questions may be raised with respect to music, specifically concerning A.B. Marx's indebtedness to Goethe. The most thorough study of organicism in German music theory, Lotte Thaler's *Organische Form in der Musiktheorie des 19. und beginnenden 20. Jahrhunderts* (1984), skilfully shows that the Goethean notions of polarity and enhancing/raising (*Steigerung*) may be applied to Marx's theory of musical forms (Thaler 66–72), but whether the applicability of these terms is sufficient to speak of "Marx's Goethe Reception" (Thaler 66) is questionable. I myself thought so earlier, but have now my doubts. In any case, I have seen no evidence that Marx was actually familiar with Goethe's most important writings on morphology. The same holds for Thaler's belief that a *morphologisches Organismus-Modell*, inspired by Goethe's morphology (56–66), was a major force in nineteenth-century German theorizing about music, not just in the work of A.B. Marx but also in those of Hugo Riemann and others. Concrete references to Goethe's texts are scarce and Thaler herself is forced to admit that even Marx goes beyond Goethe by reintroducing into organic life a teleology adopted from Hegel (73–76).

Thaler's study is limited to German music theories, and to those held by music theoreticians (it excludes theories by composers and philosophers). But Thaler's account is important for at least two reasons: first, because it distinguishes between a variety of organicist theories, above all between the aforementioned nineteenth-century *morphologisches Organismus-Modell* and twentieth-century organicist theories of music based on an *energetisches Organismus-Modell*, which I shall discuss below. Second, Thaler argues, I believe rightly, that organicist music theories emerged in conjunction with Viennese Classical music to replace extra-musical references with an internal system of relations: organicism became the key metaphor for pure instrumental (i.e. absolute) music (Thaler 12, 67f). Musical organicism emancipated "musical technique and musical form in general" (Thaler 56), but, paradoxically, this notion of music's autonomy was imported into music theory around 1800 from biology and aesthetics. Thaler rightly remarks (130) that this formalist notion was, from the outset, a broader, cultural and non-musical one.

It would require another context to show how the aesthetic principles of organicism shaped Romantic artforms throughout much of the nineteenth century. Suffice to mention here Friedrich Schlegel's poetic notion of the "arabesque", the arabesque patterns framing the paintings of Philipp Otto Runge, Beethoven's sonata form, which, according A.B. Marx, was the supreme organic structure in music, and the various architects whose works van Eck analyzes.[6]

---

6. Apart from the mentioned Schinkel, Bötticher, and Semper, van Eck discusses the organicist architectural theories of the French "romantic Pensieners" (220–227), and Viollet-de Duc (235–40). She tags her discussion of Ruskin on to that of Coleridge, under the somewhat questionable title "Religious organicism" (180–215).

The historical picture becomes considerably more confused as we come to Modernism at the end of the nineteenth and the beginning of the twentieth centuries. Van Eck includes this period only in an Epilogue entitled "The end of a tradition" (258–78), which acknowledges the organicism of some modernist architects, such as Frank Lloyd Wright, Alvar Aalto, and the architects working in the tradition of Rudolf Steiner's anthroposophy, but finds in the work of Louis Sullivan and others a "loss of the spell" (259). Shifting from a broad and flexible approach to organicism to a restrictive one, she therefore excludes a number of artistic and architectural trends in the first half of the twentieth century that are clearly indebted to some aspect of organicism: for instance, Art Nouveau, the Amsterdam School, and the emergent national schools of architecture in Eastern European countries that had recourse to indigenous folk traditions.

Thaler takes a different approach by calling our attention to what she calls the *energetisches Organismus-Modell* in the work of August Halm, Heinrich Schenker, and Hans Mersmann. (104–29). According to the "energetic" model, music is primarily understood as motion, and as an expression of a force or will beyond the composer. Within this model, compositions can no longer be interpreted through reference to the composer's psychology or biography (Thaler 11 f). But this was already precisely at the heart of Walter Pater's critique of Coleridge:

> [What makes Coleridge's] view a one-sided one is, that in it the artist has become almost a mechanical agent: instead of the most luminous and self-possessed phase of consciousness, the associative act in art or poetry is made to look like some blindly organic process of assimilation. The work of art is likened to a living organism (Pater 80).[7]

Thaler already finds something similar in the work of Hugo Riemann, and then, more explicitly, in August Halm's and Heinrich Schenker's

---

7. For Pater, the creative process is deliberate and self-conscious: "By exquisite analysis the artist attains clearness of idea; then, through many stages of refining, clearness of expression. He moves slowly over his work, calculating the tenderest tone, and restraining the subtlest curve" (ibid. 81). Pater's criticism applies not only to Coleridge but also to a number of German critics of the nineteenth century (Abrams 173).

theories (Thaler 105–117). The history of organicism in the work of German theorists becomes thereby a path from the rational to the irrational (Thaler 130). The remark is correct, though quite paradoxical in view Schenker's enormous later impact on music analysis in the USA. We can resolve the paradox if we remember that Thaler regards Schenker's theory as irrational because it deprives the composer of rational control in composing. Music analysis is, on the other hand, not interested in the psychology of the creative act; it aims to show that the work, whatever its origins, is coherent.

Halm's theory is still close to the morphological model, but the metaphor undergoes a shift: organicism now comes to mean that themes have inherent laws: "A theme itself will tell us whether it is well grown or withered, not the author, not his willed character gives here the yardstick, but the germ of the theme, its primordial form as it were". The scale, which Halm also calls *Urform*, contains according to him a will to melodic appearance (Thaler 107). And this abstract, impersonal will acquires a dangerous ideological weight when Halm develops by means of his musical organicism the notion of a musical state (*Musikstaat*). It is no longer nature but the state that now serves as a model: "The sonata is the formula for the cooperation of many individuals, it is a macro-organism, it resembles the state."[8] Music becomes a means of education for an elite minority that voluntarily subordinates its individuality to the community. An organically developed theme is "inhuman, and hence also superhuman", because "it produces work of cosmic necessity" (Thaler 116).

Thaler regards Schenker's "doctrine of organic interconnections" (*Lehre vom organischen Zusammenhang*)[9] as perhaps the most complex and wilful compared to the other ones. For the present purposes, I can only point to some aspects that relate to its organicism. Like Halm, Schenker understood composition and musical analysis as activites in pursuit of organic laws given by nature. According to him, the overtones give music a natural foundation; each piece of music organically unfolds a primordial line (*Urlinie*). The task of

---

8. "Die Sonate [...] ist die Formel des Zusammenwirkens vieler Individuen, ist ein Organismus im grossen: sie gleicht dem Staat" (Halm *Von zwei Kulturen* 33. quoted in Thaler, 105; for a more detailed discussion of Halm's use of this metaphor see Thaler, 114–17).
9. *Neue musikalische Theorien und Phantasien.III Der Freie Satz.* p. 15.

musical analysis is to distil from the complex musical texture its primordial line. Schenker stresses "the biological factor in the life of tones", and he argues that "tones have lives of their own, more independent of the artist's pen in their vitality than one would dare to believe" (Schenker, *Harmony* XXV). Thus, in Schenker, as in Halm, the musical material has an inherent natural will and independence; we find here none of the freedom that Marx attributed to the shaping of the development section of the sonata.

Schenker's concepts of *Urlinie* and *Ursatz* are surely indebted to early twentieth-century reinterpretations (or, better, misunderstandings) of Goethe's *Urpflanze*; and, his shift from anti-organicism to organicism (see below) may well have been stimulated by the publications and reinterpretations of Goethe's morphology. The motto of the first section of Schenker's mature, organicist work *Der freie Satz* (1923) is taken from Goethe's *Farbenlehre* (Goethe, *Sämtliche Werke* 10: 11). But, as Pastille argues, the young Schenker still attributed freedom to the composer. In "*Der Geist der musikalischen Technik*", a paper serialized in 1895, he declared that "musical content is never organic [...] the composer draws from his imagination various similarities and contrasts, from which he eventually makes the best choice" (Schenker 309; Pastille 31). It was only later that Schenker eliminated the composer's creative freedom by claiming that the organic power inherent in the musical material would bring about musical form. A key passage in his *Harmony* is clearly based on Immanuel Kant's notion that the intuition of a genius is based on natural laws:

> A great talent or a man of genius, like a sleepwalker, often finds the right way [...] The superior force of truth – of Nature, as it were, — is at work, mysteriously behind his consciousness, guiding his pen, without caring in the least whether the happy artist himself wanted to do the right thing or not... (*Harmony* 60)

I have tried to show in my own relevant publications that organicism had an important role in Modernism but took different forms in the various arts and national traditions. For music proper, I shall give the examples of Arnold Schönberg, Anton Webern, and Béla Bartók below. None of the organicist music theories discussed here has any connection, as far as I can tell, with the organicism one finds in the literary theories of the Russian Formalists and the Anglo-American New Critics. Schönberg and Webern rely heavily on the German tradition, especially on Goethe's notions of morphology. Indeed, I have suggested that the strongest impact of Goethean morphology upon German culture was felt not during or shortly after his lifetime but towards the end of the nineteenth and in the early decades of the twentieth centuries. This was when his works appeared in monumental editions, and his morphology, out of favour by the mid-nineteenth century, experienced a tremendous revival. Goethe became the canonized national poet of a united Germany, and his work in science also acquired prestige. Reworking and re-opening Goethean science was at the heart of his canonization. The young Rudolf Steiner became editor of Goethe's scientific writings for the *Nationalausgabe*, a monumental library of German literature, and the equally monumental *Weimarer Sophien-Ausgabe* of Goethe's oeuvre. In 1897, he published a study of Goethe's morphological worldview and he initiated the anthroposophy movement, largely on allegedly Goethean principles. By the mid-1920s, German biologists had developed a new morphological biology based on Goethean principles. This revival of Goethean morphology forms the background not only for the aforementioned music theories of Halm, Schenker, and Webern, but also for Spengler's *Der Untergang des Abendlandes*, subtitled *Umrisse einer morphologischen Weltgeschichte*, and Günter Müller's *Morphologische Poetik*, which had racist overtones—as did a number of other morphological approaches to culture and literature, from Erwin Kolbenheyer to Horst Oppel.

3.

ORGANICIST PRINCIPLES – AN OUTLINE

MODES OF ORGANICIST DISCOURSE

With the above introductory and historical information in place, we can now attempt to establish a broader theoretical outline of organicism in terms of categories. Let us start with a distinction between 1) *structural* and 2) *narrative* organicist discourses.

Structural organicist discourses hold that the parts of a whole are not just contiguous and mechanically connected, but dynamically and organically interrelated (see the Coleridge passage cited in the preliminary considerations). If we remove a cogwheel, the machine will stop but the remaining cogwheels, shafts, and other parts remain intact. If we deprive a flower of its leaves or if we damage an animal's vital organ, all other parts will also be affected, if they cease to function the organism may die. Organic structures constitute one single unit; all parts contribute to its proper functioning. For this proper functioning, a harmonious cooperation of parts is indispensable. Organicist structural models for society fix the position of individuals in social classes or castes. More naturalistic versions of organicism assert that ethnic groups, tribes, or races are definable in terms of natural features; the human species is therefore divisible into strictly different groups. Once more, applying such natural principles to the human world implies that it is governed by ineluctable laws.

Narrative organicist discourses may rely on two different dimensions of organic life. The first dimension pertains to the life-cycle of one single organic entity, whereas the second, broader organic narrative came about with Darwin's evolutionary theory. A.B. Marx seems to talk about the former in his book on Beethoven:

> Every musical creation develops, like the organisms of nature, from a germ. This, like the germs [*Keimbläschen*] or cells in flora and fauna is a unification of two or more elements (sounds, chords, rhythmical formations) and must already be an organism in order to become an origin for organisms. Such a germ is called *motive*; every composition is based on one or more motives.[10]

In other words, useful musical motives possess an inner potential to grow or broaden out into a full-fledged composition. It remains

---

10. "Jede musikalische Schöpfung entwickelt sich gleich den Organismen der Natur aus einem Keim, der aber schon, wie die Keimbläschen oder Zellen des Pflanzen- und Thierreichs, Gestaltung, Vereinigung von zwei oder mehr Einzelheiten (Tönen, Akkorden, rhythmischen Momenten), Organismus sein muss, um Organismen den Ursprung geben zu können. Ein solcher Keim wird *Motiv* genannt; auf einem oder mehr Motiven beruht jede Komposition" (Beethoven 2: 361).

somewhat unclear, however, whether Marx is speaking about the compositional process or a dynamic that performers and score readers can identify in a completed work.

Having distinguished between modes of organicist discourses we may now turn our attention to their fields of application, especially with respect to artworks. Three such fields of application seem relevant for our purposes:

    1) Organicist Views of the Mind and of the Creative Process
    2) Organic Models of Artworks
    3) Organicist Historiographies

ORGANICIST VIEWS OF THE MIND
AND OF THE CREATIVE PROCESS

Eighteenth-century theories of the mind distinguished between various faculties, and assumed that these normally cooperated. In Kant's culminating philosophy, the imagination (*Einbildungskraft*) mediated between intuition (*Anschauung*) and understanding (*Vernunft*). Romanticism and Idealism shifted the relative weight and function of these faculties but retained them as basic categories for developing new structural organicist discourses. The paradigm for this is Coleridge's famous statement in the *Biographia Literaria*: "The poet, described in *ideal* perfection, brings the whole soul of man into activity, with the subordination of its faculties to each other, according to their relative worth and dignity. He diffuses a tone, and spirit of unity, that blends, and (as it were) *fuses*, each into each, by that synthetic and magical power, to which we have exclusively appropriated the name of imagination" (7.2, 15 f).

William Wordsworth's *The Prelude*, subtitled "Growth of a Poet's Mind", one of the greatest and most ambitious English Romantic poems, displays a narrative organicist discourse not just through its very theme, but also in the extra-textual history of its making, which has increasingly engaged critical attention since the first publication of *The Prelude* in 1850. The poet started the poem upon Coleridge's encouragement at the height of their friendship in the 1790s, and kept revising it throughout his life. In the course of the twentieth century, several early versions of the text were published, so that it has become possible to reconstruct some of the historical stages of its making. The "growth" of the poem differs radically from the thematic "Growth of a Poet's Mind". Reconstructions of this kind, familiar also to scholars of Hölderlin's poems and of a great many different musical scores, have raised not only difficult technical questions about editing and publishing, but also fundamental objections to the older view that the final text authorized by an artist (*Ausgabe letzter Hand*) — in Wordsworth's case the 1850 *Prelude*—is the most valuable one. The organicist notion of "growth" may be misleading as to value, especially if value depends on the time and place of the reader as well. Questions of this kind have led in recent decades to a revival of textual studies and the emergence of what is called "genetic criticism"—a term that, unfortunately, all too often means simply a recourse to nineteenth-century positivism.

ORGANIC MODELS OF ARTWORKS

We have seen that, according to organicism, artworks must embrace a unity in multiplicity. This coherence of artworks may, but need not, be modelled explicitly in terms of a biological organism. According to Coleridge's famous passage (a continuation of the last quoted one), the imagination "reveals itself in the balance or reconciliation of opposite or discordant qualities: of sameness, with difference; of the general, with the concrete; the idea, with the image; the individual, with the representative" (7.2:16 f). The imagination "blends and harmonizes" the variety in artworks.

In Hugo Riemann's *Die Elemente der Musikalischen Ästhetik* (1900) the same principle is stated without recourse to a biological organism: "Unity in multiplicity is time and again the demand that the contemplatively enjoying mind poses to all images that are supposed to offer aesthetic pleasure".[11] In contrast, the philosopher and scientist Gustav Theodor Fechner made biological organicism both explicit and concrete: our requirement for the perfect artwork is identical to that which we demand of perfect organisms; the exis-

---

11. "Einheit in der Mannigfaltigkeit ist immer wieder die Forderung, welche der anschauend genießende Menschengeist an all Gebilde stellt, die ihm ästhetischen Genuß gewähren sollen" (170).

tence of each part enhances our pleasure in contemplating the whole; the addition of another part would diminish that pleasure; the pleasure in the whole exceeds the pleasure offered by the parts; no other mode of interconnection would improve the work (quoted in Thaler 97 f). Guido Adler's *Stil in der Musik* (1911) goes a step further by applying the biological metaphor not only to individual artworks but to music as a whole: "Music is an organism, a sum of individual organisms whose mutual relations and dependence on each other constitutes a whole".[12]

ORGANICIST HISTORIOGRAPHIES

As sacred histories lost their appeal in the latter part of the eighteenth century, biological metaphors offered themselves as replacements. General history could now be perceived as progression, more specifically as organic growth. But since organic bodies decline and die as well as grow, the organic metaphor could also be used to outline the coming of a doomsday, or to write a history of "rise and fall". Indeed, the organicist narrative could perform a double function by speaking of the decline and fall of individuals or people taking place within what is, nevertheless, characterised as a general development of mankind as a whole. Last but not least, the organic metaphor could accommodate cyclical conceptions of history: generations of plants or animals are sequences of life cycles, comparable to those that Vico, for instance, imagined as operating in history.

All such organicist narratives apply principles of nature to human society. And since nature was believed to have inevitable laws, history also had to follow ineluctable laws. It is this "naturalizing" of history that we find in Hegel, Marx, and many others philosophers of history—all of them rightly attacked later by Karl Popper.

At the end of the eighteenth century, organicist metaphors invaded and then permeated the Enlightenment discourse on progress. And though we have become sceptical about progress, its

---

12. "Die Tonkunst ist ein Organismus, eine Summe von Einzelorganismen, die in ihren Wechselbeziehungen, in ihrer Abhängigkeit voneinander ein Ganzes bilden" (13).

characteristic organic metaphors are still with us. Indeed, they are so deeply embedded in our historical discourses that it may be all but impossible to eliminate them. We have come to use them routinely, without thinking about their implied meanings: using such dead metaphors as "development", "origin", and "growth", we usually do not mean what these terms literally connote in their primary context. Contemporary, especially Postmodern, critiques of organicist historiography often assert, for instance, that genetic theories of development always appeal to causality and continuity (cf. Wellek, *The Attack* 70–71), but such summary statements, which are meant to create space for Postmodern historiography, conveniently overlook the fact that many organicist histories have been perfectly able to accommodate over-determination and discontinuity.

Organicist premises are still highly effective in histories of the arts and culture, in part because we expect histories to go beyond plain narration and to explain why things happened the way they did—if only by way of negation. We all assume in some way that Schubert would have been inconceivable had Beethoven not been on the scene already, even though such beliefs can neither be proven or disproven. In any case, such a belief does not imply that Schubert can in some way be deduced or derived from Beethoven.

Organicism has, as I have indicated, shaped our notions of artists's biographies and the genesis of artworks and our belief that artistic œuvres grow and cohere. We can focus now on larger notions of organicism in the historiography of the arts. One organicist view assumes that artforms or genres have organically interrelated autonomous histories (hence this view ignores the other genres, the other arts, and culture in general). Such is the view we find in Guido Adler's *Stil in der Musik*: "The development of music follows intrinsic laws [...] nothing can be changed in the organic process; geniuses as well as art in general come about because of inner need".[13]

Another type of organicism manifests itself in national histories of an artform, which often attribute to their subject a national

---

13. "Die Entwicklung der Musik vollzieht sich nach inneren Notwendigkeiten [...] an dem organischen Fortgang läßt sich nichts ändern, aus der inneren Not entstehen die Genies, wie Kunst überhaupt" (13).

essence and coherence—at the expense of ignoring or suppressing anything which, in the view of such histories, is alien. A third type of organicist history emerges in periodization, in reifying periods like Classicism, Romanticism, or Symbolism by endowing them with autonomous organic structures and an essential core.

Organicism has shaped not only national, generic, art-specific, and period-specific histories. It is equally present in broader cultural histories that assume the organic unity of all the artistic, cultural, and even social phenomena of an age. Writing of this kind, which argues in terms of a Hegelian *Zeitgeist*, has become discredited and replaced with case studies, examinations of a micro field. Yet even case studies cannot quite escape the problems of organicism. To be sure, a single case may be studied on the micro level, without global hermeneutic assumptions, but sooner or later, some generalizations will have to be made, and these will inevitably involve a *synecdoche*, the figure that endows the individual case with the power of a paradigm (*pars pro toto*). In criticism, this formalist theory leads to the widely discussed and practiced hermeneutic method, which proclaims that interpretation should shuttle back and forth between the parts and the whole, but even this method makes assumptions about the interrelation of parts.

Traditional studies that link artists to their age may use synech-dochic organicism without reflecting on its implications. Judith Frigyesi's highly interesting *Béla Bartók and Turn-of-the-Century Budapest* (1998) makes, for instance, two fascinating organicist claims: 1) Bartók and turn-of-the-century Budapest are organically interconnected, and 2) Bartók's and Budapest's particular organicist ideology are distinct from organicist notions elsewhere. According to Frigyesi, Bartók's music represents a specifically Hungarian variant of modernist organicism. By studying Bartók in his cultural milieu, Frigyesi takes therefore a cross-disciplinary approach to Modernism as well as to organicism. But her analyses of Bartók's music, interesting though they are, do not establish that *fin-de-siècle* Budapest culture constituted an organic unity. In spite of her efforts, Frigyesi cannot make a convincing case for her claim that Bartók's and Georg Lukács's standpoints were similar if not the same. The organicist image of Hungarian culture ignores the serious tensions that existed in Hungarian Modernism between urbanist-cosmopolitan trends and a populist search for native "organic" roots. As we shall see below, the non-Hungarian Modernist composers Schönberg and Webern also differed among themselves, although each of them espoused a specific variant of organicism.

4.

THREE MODERNIST AND ORGANICIST CONCEPTS OF MUSIC

FORMALIST ORGANICISM: ARNOLD SCHÖNBERG

Formalist organicism need not rely on exterior images from the plant or animal kingdoms. In Stephen Pepper's formulation of the formalist-organicist principle, a whole has an organic unity, when "no detail can be removed or altered without marring or even destroying the value of the whole" (79). In aesthetic terms, any change or intervention will diminish the value of a great (or perfect) artwork (Lord 263; following Osborne). A.B. Marx gives a variant of this conception in *Die Lehre von der musikalischen Komposition* by insisting on the autonomy of the arts: "art exists only for its own sake and subjected only to its own rules; it can accept only those laws and rules that follow from its own essence".[14]

This formalist-organicist credo is evident in a passage that Arnold Schönberg wrote in a key work of Modernism: Vassily Kandinsky's and Franz Marc's *Der blaue Reiter* (1912). Schönberg claims here that he used to be ignorant of the words of many Schubert songs, but once he looked at them he discovered that his earlier intuitive grasp was superior to any understanding that analysis could have yielded. Indeed, whenever he set to music texts of which he understood only the very first words, the result was always a perfect match. This proved to him that the first words of

---

14. "die Kunst ist nur um ihrer selbst willen da und sich selber Gesetz, sie kann nur das als Gesetz und Regel auf sich nehmen, was aus ihrem eignen Wesen folgt" (2).

poems constituted a perfect organic microcosm of the whole and that, in songs, the music and words were organically interrelated:

> ...artworks are like all perfect organisms. They are so homogeneous in their composition that every smallest detail reveals their true inner essence. [...] Hearing a line of a poem or a measure of a piece of music one can grasp the totality. Just as a word, a glance, a gesture, a gait, even the color of the hair, is sufficient to recognize the essence of a person. (74)

Note that Schönberg underwrites here two kinds of organicist tenets: the first claims that a poem or a piece of music is an organic whole; the second that this organic totality can be brought into another, composite, organic unity which unites words and music in a *lied* (or, for that matter, in an opera). Schönberg thus claims that the artistic process is intuitive and irrational, which corresponds to Schenker's remark that the artist-genius is a "sleepwalker". But whereas Schönberg leaves it at that, Schenker goes a step further by attributing, in the manner of Kant, the governing force to nature.

MORPHOLOGICAL AESTHETICS: ANTON WEBERN

In 1932–33, Webern gave a series of private lectures, which were later reconstructed from the notes of a listener and published posthumously under the title *Wege zur neuen Musik*. In these lectures, Webern claimed that in works of art, as in nature, necessity and law dominate: "We shall have to make efforts to ascertain what is lawful in masterworks. No trace of arbitrariness! Nothing imaginary!" (13). According to a radical version of this argument, aesthetic laws and natural laws coincide: rules in the arts are based on laws in nature.

Webern's *Wege zur neuen Musik* explicitly acknowledged its debt to Goethe's aesthetics and morphology, which Webern discovered in the 1920s (Wübbolt 104f). According to Webern, Goethe saw art "as product of general nature in the special form of human nature. This means that no significant contrast exists between products of nature and products of art, but that they are one and the same; that what we regard as an artwork and call by that name is basically nothing other than a product of general nature". Indeed, Webern claimed that the rules of art are rooted in the laws of nature—rather than in Goethe's morphology.

The claim that art has its own "natural laws" is made more frequently in music theory than in studies of literature. But the views diverge even within music, and not only because proponents of aleatory music dissent from the premises of organicism. The last quoted passage even separates Webern even from his mentor, Schönberg. The former accepted Jean-Philippe Rameau's theory that the overtones provided the natural foundations for Western tonal music (13), whereas Schönberg explicitly denied this in the introduction to his *Theory of Harmony*: the so-called *eternal laws* of music are merely empirical ones, based on our limited experiences. Tonality is no natural, eternally valid, law of music (8–9). If artistic laws existed, then, like nature's laws, they would not tolerate exceptions. Although Schönberg does not explicitly deny that such laws might be found, he was highly sceptical about them: "Attempts to explain artistic matters exclusively on natural grounds will continue to founder for a long time to come" (10f). Bartók's non-Hungarian colleagues, *pace* Frigyesi, did not share a common organicist credo.

THE ORGANICISM OF FOLK ART: BÉLA BARTÓK

Bartók once remarked: [Schönberg] "is free from all peasant influence and his complete alienation from Nature, which of course I do not regard as a blemish, is no doubt the reason why many find his work so difficult to understand" (*Essays* 326). Is the charge of "difficult to understand" not meant, after all, to show a "blemish" in Schönberg's music? Whatever the answer, Bartók did embrace the "peasant influence", which was his way to try to overcome that alienation from nature which he perceived in Schönberg and other Modernists. Two passages are relevant here. One is from a letter he wrote on August 15, 1905 to Irmy Jurkovics, which reveals some chauvinistic and anti-Semitic impulses in the decision to go into the countryside with Zoltán Kodály to rediscover the genuine roots of Hungarian folksongs:

A real Hungarian music can originate only if there is a real *Hungarian* gentry. This is why the Budapest public is so absolutely hopeless. The place has attracted a haphazardly heterogeneous, rootless group of Germans and Jews; they make up the majority of Budapest's population. It's a waste of time trying to educate them in a national spirit. Much better to educate the [Hungarian] provinces. (*Letters* 50)

This populist and nationalist perspective (so radically different from Georg Lukács's German-Jewish orientation) is a manifestation of the nineteenth-century Hungarian national awakening, which persisted among patriotic writers and intellectuals after the establishment of the Austro-Hungarian Monarchy in 1867. Bartók soon abandoned the dangerous views to which many populist artists and intellectuals succumbed in the early twentieth century throughout Eastern Europe — and elsewhere. But an important residue of Romantic naturalism survived in his worldview. In the last years of his life, in American exile, he would still believe that peasant culture was rooted in nature. As late as 1943 he would idealize the peasants by claiming that there has never been "the slightest trace of hatred or animosity against each other among those people. [...] hatred against their brothers is fostered only by the higher circles!" (*Essays* 34). It was this moral admiration that led him to regard folk music as a product of nature:

Peasant music, in the strict sense of the word, must be regarded as a natural phenomenon; the forms in which it manifests itself are due to the instinctive *transforming power* of a community entirely devoid of erudition. It is just as much a natural phenomenon as, for instance, the various manifestations of Nature in fauna and flora. (*Essays* 321)

... peasant music of this kind actually is nothing but the outcome of changes wrought by a natural force whose operation is unconscious in men who are not influenced by urban culture. (*Essays* 6)

Note that both the early and the late remarks are manifestations of organicism, different though they may be in the way they inflect it. What Bartók admires in the all but lost peasant culture is a presumed unity and harmony between members of the peasant society, as well as between human beings and the soil, that is lacking in the fragmented and decadent urban culture.

5.

THE DEATH OF ORGANICISM?

I started out with recent critiques of organicism in the history and theory of music. To those of Kerman and Norris, I could have added critiques by Ruth Solie, Rose Rosengard Subotnik, Allan Street, Lydia Goehr, and many others, including my own. These critiques of organicism in music dovetail with more philosophical critiques of organicism by Roland Barthes, Michel Foucault, Jacques Derrida, Stanley Fish, Richard Rorty and many others. Postmodernism could also be called post-organicism, for Postmodern thinkers are opposed to reifications of culture, and to the imposition of unity and identity upon cultural matters that they regard as ambiguous, multi-faceted, contradictory, and full of discontinuities. Michel Foucault, for instance, questions the notions of author and œuvre that are defined, explicitly or otherwise, by means of an organicist vocabulary, and he has attacked with great vigour the tradition of *Geistesgeschichte*, which speaks of harmonious unities and smooth transitions. Indeed, one need not be a Postmodern thinker to be aware of the pernicious results of a nationalism that excludes or suppresses in the name of an organic national unity whatever it considers alien, decadent, or simply other.

An appropriately organicist epitaph for organicist theory might then read as follows: "Organicism was born in the Romantic period, flourished in the nineteenth and early twentieth centuries, and died in the Postmodern era". And yet, organicism is older than Romanticism and may outlive Postmodernism, for it is too multifarious to be condemned wholesale. Whoever does so becomes automatically guilty of reducing, in what is itself an organicist manner, a complicated and multifaceted concept. Indeed, manifestations of organicism are still (or, perhaps, once again) around us everywhere: witness forms of holism, the Whole Earth Movement, the Gaya hypothesis, or the revival of interest in the *Gesamtkunstwerk*. I have therefore taken the liberty to package my paper—tongue in cheek, to be sure—in the wrappings of an organicist narrative about birth, growth, and decline—but not death. While certain forms of organicism have died or will die, others resist, and yet others are only just coming about. Stephen Pepper may ultimately be right that organicism is an enduring "world hypothesis".

WORKS CITED

- Abrams, M. H. *The Mirror and the Lamp*. London: Oxford UP, 1953.
- Adler, Guido. *Stil in der Musik*. 1911. 2nd ed. 1929. Rpt. Wiesbaden 1973.
- Appel, Toby. *The Cuvier-Geoffroy Debate. French Biology in the Decades Before Darwin*. New York and Oxford: Oxford UP, 1987.
- Bartók, Béla. *Béla Bartók Essays*. Ed. Benjamin Suchoff. London: Faber & Faber, 1976.
- Bartók, Béla. *Letters*. Collected, Selected, Edited and Annotated by János Demény. Budapest: Corvina Press, 1971.
- Benziger, James. "Organic Unity: Leibniz to Coleridge." *PMLA* 66 (1951): 24–48.
- Coleridge, Samuel Taylor. *Collected Works*. 16 vols. General editor Kathleen Coburn. Princeton: Princeton UP, 1969–.
- Eck, Caroline van. *Organicism in 19th-Century Architecture: an Inquiry into its Theoretical and Philosophical Background*. Amsterdam: Architectura & Natura, 1994.
- Frigyesi, Judit. "Béla Bartók and the Concept of Nation and Volk in Modern Hungary." *The Musical Quarterly* 78/2 (1994): 255–87.
- Frigyesi, Judit. *Béla Bartók and Turn-of-the-Century Budapest*. Berkeley: U of California P, 1998.
- Goethe, Johann Wolfgang. *Sämtliche Werke nach Epochen seines Schaffens [Münchner Ausgabe]*. 22 vols. Ed. Karl Richter. München: Hanser, 1985–1998.
- Halm, August. *Von zwei Kulturen der Musik*. (1913) 3rd. ed. Stuttgart: Klett, 1947.
- Kerman, Joseph. *Musicology*. London: Fontana, 1985.
- Marx, A[dolf] B[ernhard]. *Ludwig van Beethoven. Leben und Schaffen*. 2 vols. 2nd ed. Berlin: Otto Jahnke, 1863.
- Marx, A[dolf] B[ernhard]. *Die Lehre von der musikalischen Komposition*. 4th ed. Leipzig, 1852.
- Müller, Günther. *Morphologische Poetik*. Edited by Elena Müller. Darmstadt: Wissenschaftliche Buchgesellschaft, 1968.
- Müller-Sievers, Helmut. *Epigenesis: Naturphilosophie im Sprachdenken Wilhelm von Humboldts*. Paderborn: Schöningh, 1993.
- Müller-Sievers, Helmut. *Self-Generation. Biology, Philosophy, and Literature Around 1800*. Stanford: Stanford UP, 1997.
- Neubauer, John. "Epigenetische Literaturgeschichten bei August und Wilhelm Schlegel." *Kunst—die andere Natur*. Ed. Reinhard Wegner. Göttingen: Vandenhoeck & Ruprecht, 2004. 211–227.
- Neubauer, John. "Modernisme en organicisme." *Literatuurwetenschap tussen betrokkenheid en distantie*. Ed. Liesbeth Korthals Altes and Dick Schram. Assen: Van Gorcum, 2000. 51–60.
- Neubauer, John. "Morphological Poetics?" *Style* 22 (1988): 263–274.
- Neubauer, John. "Organic Form in Romantic Theory: The Case of Goethe's Morphology." *Romanticism across the Disciplines*. Ed. by Larry H. Peer. Lanham: UP of America, 1998. 207–230.
- Neubauer, John. Rev. of Judith Frigyesi, *Béla Bartók and Turn-of-the-Century Budapest*. Berkeley: U of California P, 1998. *Nexus*. Nr. 22, 135–39.
- Norris, Christopher. "Deconstruction, Musicology and Analysis: some Recent Approaches in Critical Review." *Thesis Eleven* 56 (1999): 107–118.

– Orsini, G.N.G. "The Organic Concepts in Aesthetics." *Comparative Literature.* 21 (1969): 1–30.
– Orsini, G.N.G. "Organicism." *Dictionary of the History of Ideas.* Ed. in chief Philip P. Wiener. 5 vols. N.Y.: Scribner's, 1973–74. 3: 421–27.
– Pastille, William A. "Schenker, Anti-Organicist." *19th-Century Music* 8 (1984): 33–34.
– Pater, Walter. "Coleridge." *Works.* Vol. 5. London: Macmillan, 1901.
– Pepper, Stephen. *World Hypotheses. A Study of Evidence.* 1948. Berkeley: U of California P, 1970.
– Riemann, Hugo. *Die Elemente der Musikalischen Ästhetik.* Berlin, Stuttgart, 1900.
– Schenker, Heinrich. "Der Geist der musikalischen Technik." *Musikalisches Wochenblatt* 26 (1895): 245–46, 257–59, 273–74, 279–80, 297–98, 309–10, 325–26.
– Schenker, Heinrich. *Harmony.* 1906. Oswald Jonas, ed.; Elizabeth Mann Borgese, trans. Chicago: U of Chicago P, 1954.
– Schenker, Heinrich. *Neue musikalische Theorien und Phantasien. III Der freie Satz.* Oswald Jonas, ed. 2nd ed. Vienna: Universal Edition, 1956.
– Schlegel, August Wilhelm. *Vorlesungen über dramatische Kunst und Literatur.* 1811. 2 vols. Ed. Giovanni Vittorio Amoretti. Bonn: Kurt Schroeder, 1923.
– Schönberg, Arnold. *Theory of Harmony.* 1911/1940. Trans. by Roy E. Carter. London: Faber, 1978.
– Schönberg, Arnold. "Das Verhältnis zum Text." *Der blaue Reiter.* Ed. Wassily Kandinsky and Franz Marc. Munich: Pieper, 1912. 60–75.
– Solie, Ruth. "The Living Work: Organicism and Musical Analysis." *19th-Century Music* 4 (1980): 147–56.
– Spengler, Oswald. *Der Untergang des Abendlandes. Umrisse einer morphologischen Weltgeschichte.* 1917–23. Munich: Beck, 1981.
– Steiner, Rudolf. *Goethes Weltanschauung.* 1897. Berlin: Philosophisch-Anthroposophischer Verlag, 1918.
– Thaler, Lotte. *Organische Form in der Musiktheorie des 19. und beginnenden 20. Jahrhunderts.* Munich, Salzburg: Katzbichler, 1984.
– Webern, Anton. *Wege zur neuen Musik.* Ed. by Willi Reich. Vienna: Universal Edition, 1960.
– Wellek, René. *The Attack on Literature.* Chapel Hill: U of North Carolina P, 1982.
– Wubbolt, Georg. "Weberns Goethe-Rezeption: Ein Beitrag zum Thema Natur und Kunst." *Opus Anton Webern.* Ed. Dieter Rexroth. Berlin: Quadriga, 1983.

BEETHOVEN'S
"BRIDGETOWER" SONATA, OP. 47

Janet Schmalfeldt

Excitement has long surrounded accounts of the première of Beethoven's *Sonata for Piano and Violin in A, Op. 47.* We have it directly from Beethoven's pupil Ferdinand Ries that, in the early morning hours of May 24, 1803, Beethoven summoned him to copy the violin part of the first movement as fast as possible; Beethoven's performance, with the renowned virtuoso violinist, George Augustus Polgreen Bridgetower, was to occur at 8 o'clock in the Vienna Augartensaal. Ries reports that the piano score was "noted down only here and there" and that Bridgetower had to perform the second movement that morning from the manuscript —presumably by reading it from over Beethoven's shoulder— because "there was no time to copy it".[1] Best of all, Beethoven and Bridgetower must surely have given their audience an astounding display of spontaneity and camaraderie. Bridgetower recounts that, within the repeat of the first movement's exposition, at the fermata in bar 27, he imitated, thus anticipating, the pianist's cadenza—the C-major arpeggio—in bar 36 (see Example 4a). Beethoven was so pleased that he jumped up, embraced Bridgetower, and said, "Noch einmal, mein lieber Bursch!" ("Once again, my dear boy!"). He then held the *sostenuto* pedal as Bridgetower repeated the cadenza.[2]

Ries, Bridgetower himself, Carl Czerny, and Anton Schindler have all asserted unequivocally that Beethoven composed his Op. 47

1. Franz Gerhard Wegeler and Ferdinand Ries, *Biographische Notizen über Beethoven* (Coblenz, 1838), 82–83; as cited in Alexander Thayer, *Thayer's Life of Beethoven*, rev. and ed. Elliot Forbes (Princeton: Princeton University Press, 1976), 332.
2. See Thayer, *Thayer's Life of Beethoven*, 333. Within my presentation in Ghent of the original version of this essay, at the International Orpheus Academy for Music Theory 2005, violinist Ann Vancoillie brilliantly reenacted Bridgetower's improvised cadenza and performed many other excerpts from the first movement of Op. 47 with me. I am profoundly grateful to Ms. Vancoillie for her willingness to collaborate with me in that presentation, and I thank the Orpheus Institute for having arranged for her to do this.

sonata for Bridgetower.[3] Elliot Forbes has disagreed. In his 1967 revised edition of Alexander Thayer's Beethoven biography, Forbes argues that the sketches for the first and second movements, to be found in the last pages of the Wielhorsky sketchbook, date from "early 1803", thus prior to Bridgetower's arrival in Vienna later that spring. Forbes concludes that "at the start of its composition Beethoven did not have Bridgetower in mind".[4] As a sample of the Op. 47 sketches from the Wielhorsky sketchbook, excerpts from the first page of these have been reproduced at Example 1. Note that many of the essential elements of the first movement, including those treacherous broken thirds for the pianist in the development section, are already much in evidence.

Example 1. From the Wielhorsky sketchbook, Kniga eskizov Beethoven za 1802–1803 gody [Ein Skizzenbuch Beethovens von 1802–1803], *ed. Natan Fischmann (Moskow, 1962). Formal annotations added.*

---

3. As cited in Sieghard Brandenburg, "Zur Textgeschichte von Beethovens Violinsonate Opus 47", *Musik, Edition, Interpretation: Gedenkschrift Gunthers Henle,* ed. Martin Bente (Munich: Henle, 1980), 111. Others have claimed in passing, but without further discussion, that Beethoven wrote his Op. 47 Sonata for Bridgetower; see, for example, Josephine R. B. Wright, "George Polgreen Bridgetower: An African Prodigy in England 1789–99", *Musical Quarterly* 66 (1980): 65; Ann-Louise Coldicott, "Beethoven's Musical Environment", in *The Beethoven Compendium: A Guide to Beethoven's Life and Music,* ed. Barry Cooper (London: Thames and Hudson, 1991), 88–89; and Barry Cooper, "Who's Who of Beethoven's Contemporaries", in *The Beethoven Compendium,* 43.
4. Elliot Forbes, in *Thayer's Life of Beethoven,* 333.

In 1980 Sieghard Brandenburg challenged Elliot Forbes's view. Brandenburg's complex reassessment of the Wielhorsky sketchbook need not be rehearsed here, but his argument warrants our consideration: namely, given that Beethoven's sketches for Op. 47 can be assigned a later date and Bridgetower's arrival in Vienna an earlier one, the likelihood that they had already met before Beethoven began composing Op. 47 is strong. As Brandenburg says: "It is difficult to accept that a violin sonata constructed in such a completely concertante manner would have come into being uninfluenced by the violinistic qualities of that very violinist by whom it was performed for the first time."[5] Brandenburg's conclusions about the genesis of Op. 47 have not, to my knowledge, been refuted; nor, however, have their ramifications been fully explored.

Elsewhere I have examined Carl Dahlhaus's claim that the *processual character of form* in the first movement of Beethoven's "Tempest" *Piano Sonata, Op. 31, No. 2*, defines the "new paths", or "a wholly new style", that Beethoven determined to explore around the year 1802.[6] Within the year that followed, no works after the Op. 31 sonatas save for the "Eroica" Variations, Op. 35, and the Violin Sonata, Op. 47, more fully substantiate the idea that Beethoven had found his new path. Nor would Beethoven ever again compose an accompanied sonata "scritta in uno stile molto concertante, quasi come d'un concerto" ("written in a very concertante style, almost like that of a concerto"), as he put it—a work of unparalleled virtuosity and fire for both players. Indeed, even the first reviewer of Op. 47 in the *Allgemeine Musikalische Zeitung* saw subsequent performances as dependent upon the coming together of "two virtuosi to whom nothing remains difficult, who possess so much spirit and understanding that, with practice, they could write similar works themselves".[7] Like Brandenburg, I should like to believe that we

---

5. Brandenburg, "Zur Textgeschichte," 113. My translation, with the gracious help of my colleague Mark DeVoto.
6. See Janet Schmalfeldt, "Form as the Process of Becoming: The Beethoven–Hegelian Tradition and the 'Tempest' Sonata", *Beethoven Forum* 4 (1995): 37–71.
7. From the *Allgemeine musikalische Zeitung*, 28 August 1805, cols. 769–72; as cited in Suhnne Ahn, "Beethoven's Opus 47: Balance and Virtuosity", *The Beethoven Violin Sonatas: History, Criticism, Performance*, ed. Lewis Lockwood and Mark Kroll (Urbana and Chicago: University of Illinois Press, 2004), 81n.18.

can attribute this remarkable composition most especially to the coming together of Beethoven and Bridgetower.

What can we know about George Augustus Polgreen Bridgetower? A mere seven-page biographical sketch by one F. G. Edwards, published in the *Musical Times* in 1909, served as Thayer's sole source of information; for Josephine R. B. Wright in 1980, Edwards' account remained "the most comprehensive study of Bridgetower".[8] From Edwards we learn that Bridgetower may have been born in Biala, Poland, to a Polish mother, and that his father, like him, was known as "the African prince".[9] Edwards proposes 1779 as the approximate year of Bridgetower's birth. In his 2005 monograph, Clifford D. Panton supplies the birth-year as 1778, making Bridgetower eight years younger than Beethoven.[10] Panton is right to stress that this person of colour, whose father is said to have been Abyssinian (Ethiopian) from the West Indies, came into the world "during the famous slave trade triangle that existed... between Europe, the African continent and the Americas", and at a time when negative images of black people had begun to abound in Europe.[11] Reviews from Paris and then England (Bath, then London) permit Edwards to establish beyond question that already, by the late 1780s, Bridgetower's elegant, accomplished father had succeeded in displaying his son as an astonishingly brilliant child prodigy; for example, in the *Bath Chronicle* of December 3, 1789, it is reported of "Master Bridgtower" [sic] that his "taste and execution on the violin [are] equal, perhaps

---

8. F. G. Edwards, "George P. Bridgetower and the Kreutzer Sonata", *Musical Times* 49 (1908): 302–308; Wright, "Bridgetower: An African Prodigy", 67.

9. Edwards, "George P. Bridgetower," 302–303.

10. Clifford D. Panton, *George Augustus Polgreen Bridgetower, Violin Virtuoso and Composer of Color in Late 18th Century Europe* (New York: Edwin Mellen Press, 2005), 8. As acknowledged by Panton, Bridgetower's correct year of birth was confirmed by Betty Matthews, Honorary Archivist for the Royal Society of Musicians (Betty Matthews, "Letters to the Editor: George Bridgetower", *The Musical Times* 122 [1981], 85).

11. Panton, *Bridgetower*, 5–6, 19–22. As cited by Wright ("Bridgetower: An African Prodigy", 68–69), Hans Volkmann provided evidence that Bridgetower's father probably emigrated, or escaped, to Europe from Barbados (Volkmann, *Beethoven in seinen Beziehungen zu Dresden* [Dresden, 1942], 151). Wright and Panton point out that the name Bridgetower suggests the Barbados seaport of Bridgetown (see Panton, *Bridgetower*, 5). As Panton says, "... it would have been very natural for an African to adopt the name of either a place or a family to which he may have been sold" (6).

superior, to the best professor of the present or any former day".[12] From the very outset, moreover, it would seem that race would be an issue for Bridgetower. The 1789 review in *Le Mercure de France* of his début in Paris, as a "jeune Nègre des Colonies", includes the following observation: "His talent, as genuine as it is precocious, is one of the best replies one can give to the philosophers who wish to deprive those of his nation and his color the faculty of distinguishing themselves in the arts." [13]

By the time the 25-year-old George Bridgetower met up with Beethoven, he had long ago taken London by storm and performed concertos with Haydn (in 1791, 1792, and 1794), with whom he may have studied when his father was serving as Prince Nicolas Esterházy's personal page at the Esterházy estate in Eisenstadt.[14] He had won the patronage of the Prince of Wales (later to become George IV); he had gained the esteem and friendship of leading musicians in London, including the violinist-composer Viotti; with letters of introduction from the English court and from Dresden, he was about to achieve a "most brilliant reception among the highest musical circles" in Vienna.[15] In fact, on May 18, 1803, shortly before his concert with Bridgetower, Beethoven himself sent an introductory letter on Bridgetower's behalf to Baron Alexander Wetzlar.[16] It is tempting to wonder whether, when Beethoven and Bridgetower met for the first time, they might have seen themselves in one another. In the engraving of Beethoven from around 1801 by Johann Joseph Neidl, after a drawing by Gandolph Ernst Stainhauser von Treuberg, Beethoven bears a notable resemblance to Bridgetower looking roughly the same age, as portrayed in a miniature attributed to Chinnery.[17] Beethoven

---

12. Edwards, "George P. Bridgetower", 303.
13. Ibid. "Son talent, aussi vrai que précose, est une des meilleures réponses que l'on puisse faire aux Philosophes qui veulent priver ceux de sa Nation et de sa couleur, de la faculté de se distinguer dans les Arts."
14. See Wright, "Bridgetower: An African Prodigy", 79, 70.
15. Edwards, "George P. Bridgetower", 305.
16. Beethoven, *The Letters of Beethoven*, trans. and ed. Emily Anderson, 3 vols. (London: Macmillan, 1961), vol. 1, No. 74 (p. 75).
17. Neidl's engraving of Beethoven, located in the Beethoven–Haus Bonn, has been reproduced in Maynard Solomon, *Beethoven*, 2nd rev. ed. (New York: Schirmer Books). The portrait of Bridgetower is located in the British Library (BL PP 1931 1pcx (vol. 182, p. 296) and can be viewed on its website.

was often described as dark-eyed and dark-complexioned: at home in Bonn as a young boy he was called *der Spagnol* (the Spaniard); Thayer, recalling the anecdote that Prince Esterházy referred to Haydn as "a Moor", speculates that Beethoven "had even more of the Moor in his looks" than Haydn.[18] But whether or not a shared sense of "otherness", of being marked as "different", or "foreign", might have drawn these two men together, most pertinent here is the possibility that in Bridgetower Beethoven met his match as a performer —a virtuoso of the magnitude for which he himself had won his earliest renown, and one who, like himself, could not only dazzle but move his listeners to tears.[19] Here was someone for whom Beethoven could compose the most brilliant, technically demanding, and passionate violin sonata of his own career, and perhaps of all time.

That Beethoven's "new path" involved an intensive, maybe even obsessive, attention to molecular-like, often pitch-specific motives as generative forces surely finds confirmation in most writings about Op. 47; for example, the analyses of Rudolph Réti and Owen Jander hinge almost exclusively on this facet of the first movement, although the generative elements they identify are not the same.[20] Little effort, on the other hand, has been made to consider just how the composer's taut motivic network interacts with his phrase-structural, tonal, and mid-level formal processes to create such an enormous expansion of his first movement's sonata form—one that seems especially conceived to enhance the effect of a fabulous dialogue between two musical soul-mates in the heat of an exchange. Réti appears unaware that the finale of Op. 47 was composed first, but both he and Jander propose connections among all three movements. For Suhnne Ahn,

---

18. Thayer, *Thayer's Life of Beethoven*, 72, 134.
19. See Solomon, *Beethoven*, 77–79. Thayer quotes Carl Czerny (in his contribution to Cocks's *London Musical Miscellany*, August 2, 1852) as follows: "In whatever company he might chance to be, [Beethoven] knew how to produce such an effect upon every hearer that frequently not an eye remained dry, while many would break out into loud sobs; for there was something wonderful in his expression in addition to the beauty and originality of his ideas and his spirited style of rendering them" (Thayer, *Thayer's Life of Beethoven*, 185).
20. Rudolph Réti, *Thematic Patterns in Sonatas of Beethoven*, ed. Deryck Cooke (New York: Da Capo Press, 1992; orig. publ., New York: Macmillan, 1967), chap. 14, "The Thematic Pitch of the *Kreutzer* Sonata", 145–65; Owen Jander, "The 'Kreutzer' Sonata as Dialogue", *Early Music* 16 (1988): 34–49.

Example 2. Beethoven, Sonata in A for Piano and Violin, Op. 47, 1st mvt. (mm. 1–18).

"the finale generates most of the ideas for the entire work", and yet the evidence she provides for this view is meagre.[21] In short, a new consideration of the Op. 47 Sonata is warranted. I focus in particular

---

21. Ahn, "Beethoven's Opus 47", 64. See also Suhnne Ahn, "Genre, Style, and Compositional Procedure in Beethoven's 'Kreutzer' Sonata, Opus 47" (Ph.D. diss., Harvard University, 1997).

upon some of the technical, motivic, and formal challenges that the violinist and pianist share on an utterly equal footing in the first movement—details that all but suggest a compositional collaboration between the two.

As a first, magnanimous tribute to his violinist, Beethoven gives the opening four-bar phrase of his Adagio introduction solely to the violin (Example 2). Never in his accompanied sonatas had he done this before, nor would he ever do it again within an Adagio opening. As the violinist negotiates the initial A-major chord, with two double stops in quick succession, sonatas of an older kind might momentarily come to mind; George Bridgetower eventually became well known for his exquisite performances *from memory* of Johann Sebastian Bach's sonatas for unaccompanied violin (recall the double-stopped openings in the Adagios of Bach's Sonatas in G minor and A minor).[22] The violinist's serene, but exceedingly difficult, opening phrase,[23] all in the tonic major, is about to establish a pattern: as the movement unfolds, it will be the violinist who consistently introduces new materials, and then the pianist who follows suit. But both in the introduction and within the slow-moving

---

22. See Samuel Wesley's appreciation of Bridgewater's performances of "the matchless and immortal solos of Sebastian Bach", as cited in Edwards, "George P. Bridgetower", 305. As of this writing, it cannot be verified that Bridgetower had already begun to perform Bach's unaccompanied sonatas, or that Beethoven knew them, by 1803. I am grateful, however, to Su Yin Mak for having placed me in touch with Benedict Cruft, violinist and Dean of Music at the School of Music, Hong Kong Academy for Performing Arts; Dean Cruft kindly informed me that Bach's unaccompanied violin sonatas were first published by Simrock in 1802, thus opening up the possibility that Bridgetower gained this first edition when he arrived on the continent that year, and thus that he might even have played some of Bach's sonatas for Beethoven.

23. To quote Max Rostal, in his *Beethoven, The Sonatas for Piano and Violin: Thoughts on their Interpretation* (trans. Horace and Anna Rosenberg; New York: Toccata Press, 1985): "For most violinists this unaccompanied beginning seems a nightmare. A rendition which is truly persuasive in its interpretation demands here enormous concentration and inner calm: like a prologue, it immediately proclaims a great work; indeed, it must announce the necessary atmosphere already with the very first chord" (120). I thank violinist Karma Tomm for offering the following technical observations about the violinist's opening phrase: string crossings between the second and third beats of bar 1 make it difficult to sustain the effect of legato; moreover, extensions in the left hand when moving between those same two beats make for difficulty in accurate intonation (fingers 1 and 2 on F#–D, to fingers 2 and 4 on D–B). In combination, these two techniques call for intense focus and control.

opening part of the first secondary theme (ST¹; see Example 4c), the pianist's varied repetition seems to serve as a gentle warning: in both cases the pianist introduces modal mixture, inflecting the minor mode as if to say, "Mein lieber Bursch, there's a more sombre side to the musical world we've begun to explore together." Moreover, in the case of both the slow introduction and the first secondary theme, the music hesitates, it takes time to reflect, it gives the impression of groping towards an outcome; in both cases, the outcome is a release of energy more ferocious than anything in Beethoven's earlier works.

As the pianist's inverted minor-subdominant chord in bar 5 moves to the dominant at bar 6, and then on to the submediant in bar 7, a second warning begins to emerge. As within so many vocal and instrumental works from the turn of the nineteenth century onwards, Beethoven will treat the semitone relationship $\hat{6}$–to–$\hat{5}$—in this case F–to–E—as his pervasive resource for local and long-range motivic continuity, on multiple levels of structure and in ever-changing formal contexts. A second pitch-specific semitone—the dyad G#–A, or $\hat{7}$–$\hat{8}$—will join forces with the F–E motive, or its more pronounced version, E–F, sometimes reinforcing its instability as a neighbour relationship, sometimes counteracting this by providing closure. Most importantly, Beethoven assigns a specific rhythmic character to the two dyads: again and again each of these will appear in the context of upbeat/downbeat, and short-long, short-long. In fact, the violinist's very first gesture—the opening double-stopped chord—anticipates this rhythmic detail. Put simply, Beethoven makes it impossible for his listeners to miss the generative role of his two dyads; he *insists* that we follow the developmental path they will take. The first appearance of the F–E motive occurs in both the treble and the bass at bars 5–6. (Here and elsewhere in my examples, I have literally "flagged" these motions, borrowing from Schenkerian analysis the practice of flagging metric neighbour tones and slurring these to their stemmed tones of resolution.) The violinist has already introduced the G#–A motion at bars 2–3; when the pianist harmonically reinterprets the violinist's melody at bars 6–7, we now hear the two semitones *simultaneously* —G#–to–A and E–to–F, moving together in parallel 10ths.

What then motivates an imitative dialogue between the two instruments (at bars 8–11) should begin to reveal itself: the violinist's entries within this exchange allow for a crescendo, first from F to E, then from A to G#, and then back to the high A-natural, at which point the pianist, now doubling the violin, again presents both dyads in 10ths. As within the pianist's first phrase, the bass at bars 12–13 again moves upward via semitone to the dominant of the mediant, C major. This time the violinist, having reached the peak of the crescendo in bar12, takes a surprising plunge downward, to the descending semitone C-to-B. First-time listeners, and maybe even later ones, cannot be expected to know that the violinist has just anticipated the *contour*, but only one of the two semitones, of the head motive in the forthcoming Presto. As Rudolph Réti has suggested, the rest of this Adagio can be interpreted as a search for the other semitone. When the pianist's E–F# (bars 13–14) becomes E–F-*natural* in bar 15, a voice exchange transfers that interval to the violinist; seven successive iterations of the E–F dyad, as supported by the pianist's tonicized subdominant, confirm that this *must* be the sought-after semitone. Now everything is in place; it is as if a spring has been coiled, and the fermatas at bar 18 caution us that it is about to be released. When that happens at bar 19, both players might experience a split second of relief; but, to paraphrase Réti, now the real work begins.

As shown at Example 3a, Réti subdivides the first phrase of the Presto into three seminal segments, which he identifies as I., *prime shape*, II., *step-ladder*, and III., *4 + 3* (ascending 4th, followed by falling 3rd). My alternative view, at Example 3b, betrays the influence of my Schenkerian training and takes a critical stand against Réti's apparent indifference both to harmonic progression and to scale degree; a consideration of these dimensions can substantiate long-range motivic voice-leading connections that Réti does not address.

For example, my reading proposes that a stepwise ascent through the interval of a seventh — <F–G#–A–B–C–D–E> (a reinterpretation of Réti's *step-ladder*) — fundamentally carries the violinist's line to the primary tone of the movement, the mediant-supported E-natural as $\hat{5}$ at the fermata.[24] Ramifications of this ascent will especially emerge within the movement's coda. The arrival on E-natural completes a long-range "composing out" of the Presto's opening E–F motive over the span of the complete phrase: as a broad neighbour tone, the F-natural at bar 19 resolves both registrally and harmonically to the E at the fermata. If Bridgetower had by chance intuited this long-range connection, no wonder he was inspired to celebrate it with his improvised cadenza at bar 27!

Example 3. (a) From Rudolph Réti, Thematic Patterns in Sonatas of Beethoven, ed. Deryck Cooke (New York: Da Capo, 1992; orig. publ., 1967), 145. (b) Alternative view.

---

24. I am indebted to William Rothstein, who, in response to an earlier version of my graph at Example 3b, kindly offered me a different view of the long-range connection from F at bar 19 to E at bar 27. I am indebted … a different view of the long-range connection from F at bar 19 to E at bar 27 — one that I attempt to represent here.. At Example 4.3b, level 2 proposes that Beethoven's actual outer-voice counterpoint is a variant of the simpler motion in which the bass ascends in 10ths with the upper voice; level 3 summarizes the fundamental progression as ii—V7—I in C (III). One remarkable implication of this reading is that the *only* structural home-tonic harmony within Beethoven's main theme is the tonic that marks the cadence at bar 44!

Let me acknowledge my respect for Rudolph Réti's *Grundgestalt*-oriented analysis of Op. 47. But I think that so much more can be gained if we consider the development of Beethoven's motivic ideas in the light of his formal processes, and so I proceed accordingly. I wish to examine how motives and phrases combine to create huge thematic structures within the exposition—ones that represent a considerable break from Classical conventions.

William Caplin has noted that the violinist's opening Adagio phrase participates as a compound basic idea (CBI) within a phrase structure that resembles a modulating sixteen-bar sentence, compressed over the span of bars 1–13.[25] In fact, the introduction's opening sentential design looks forward not only to the Presto's main theme (MT) but also to the transition and the first of the two secondary themes within the Presto movement proper. As Caplin puts it, however, "of all the large-scale units of classical form, slow introductions are the least predictable in their organization".[26] In this case, the introduction, though characteristically hesitant and ultimately unstable, opens with the clearest, most conventional formal design of the movement as a whole. The enormous, highly individualized sentences that follow will expand upon the general pattern and dynamic of a sentence in completely unprecedented ways.

For example, in virtually every one of Beethoven's earlier violin and cello sonatas, one can find an opening theme, sometimes in more than one movement, that gives each instrument a chance to present the initial phrase or phrase-group. These "equal opportunity" openings tend to take the form of simple main-theme repetitions, or antecedent-consequents, or written-out varied repetitions within small binaries, or repetitions that retrospectively become the beginning of a transition. To my knowledge, the main theme of Op. 47 strikes upon an entirely new path, comparable in part only to the opening of the "Tempest". The violinist takes the lead

25. William E. Caplin, *Classical Form: A Theory of Formal Functions for the Music of Haydn, Mozart, and Beethoven* (New York: Oxford University Press, 1998), 207–208. Caplin notes that: "Problematic in this interpretation, of course, is the lack of tonic prolongation at the end of the presentation" (207). The same must be said for the presentation (at bars 19–36) within Beethoven's Presto main theme.
26. Ibid., 203.

at the beginning of the Presto (Example 4a), but what seems at first like an imperfect authentic cadence in the "wrong" key—the mediant—concludes the phrase at the fermata in bar 27.

Example 4a. Op. 47, 1st mvt. (Exposition, mm. 19–45).

Now it is the pianist's turn, but the same "wrong" goal is achieved at the cadenza in bar 36. The fermatas have the effect of bringing the thematic process to highly unusual halts—moments of reflection and then showing-off that seem to prevent a genuine "main theme" from taking shape. Given that main themes, by definition, close in the home key, neither of the two closures in the mediant can serve to bring this theme to completion; something else will be needed. Beethoven's solution is to create a heightened *continuation* phrase—one that invites us retrospectively to interpret the two preceding phrases as compound basic ideas within a massive *presentation*. In coordination with the pianist's new, driving, continuous quaver motion, the compression of the continuation creates the effect of urgency. A most striking feature of the continuation, moreover, is its motivic content. Having opened with the seminal <E–F—A–G#> idea, the violinist begins again at bars 37–38 with the E–F semitone; here, and for the first of several times to come, the motive appears in a new harmonic guise. Now an ascending-step sequence allows the motive to strive upward chromatically, until, at the apex of the phrase, the counterpart semitone G#–A provides the climax and then brings closure into the first and only genuine authentic cadence, elided (?) at bar 45.

It would be hard to imagine a more purely violinistic figure in 1803 than the one with which the transition begins (Example 4b). Beethoven seems determined to put Bridgetower physically to work in the most strenuous, and most visually exciting, way—via repeated, continuous string crossing. From his first Piano Sonata onward, Beethoven had certainly written hundreds of bars of broken octaves for the piano—"murky bass", as it is called, and variants of this. The specific octave gestures that the violinist and pianist exchange at the beginning of the transition are new to the piano; they have been so clearly inspired by the violin. As another lengthy sentential structure now gets underway, we can note that these gestures are also the product of motivic thought: the violinist's two-bar tonic-oriented pattern, imitated by the pianist to create a four-bar unit, provides a new sub-metric neighbour-tone setting for the G#–A semitone; the dominant-oriented response at bars 49–51 gives the pianist a lightning opportunity to highlight the neighbour-motion E–F–E over the bar line. The eight-bar unit heard thus far

Example 4b. Op. 47, 1st mvt. (Exposition, mm. 45–78.)

could well have served as a simple presentation within a sixteen-bar sentence; but the "equal opportunity" tradition yields a repetition of the entire eight bars, with the two performers exchanging roles. As within the main theme—and especially in light of this devilish Presto tempo, which clearly suggests "hyper-measures", in the sense of two notated bars standing for only one real bar—the eight-bar repetition sounds more like a repeated CBI than like a repeated pre-sentation. What follows confirms that impression: this time the continuation will nearly balance the sixteen-bar presentation; it will be a thrilling twelve-bar unit in which an ascending-step sequence and *sforzandos* on the off-beats lead to a climactic arrival on the dominant of the new key, E minor (= v), at bar 73. At the begin-ning of the overpowering eighteen-bar "standing-on-the-dominant" that ensues, Réti hears a reference in the violin part to his *prime shape*, the head motive of the main theme, now transposed and with the two dyads reversed. Whether or not Réti's view is persuasive, we can surely agree that this passage offers a striking anticipation of the transition Beethoven was to compose for his "Waldstein" Sonata just six or seven months later.

As the goal of the transition, the beginning of Beethoven's first secondary theme could not possibly provide greater contrast (Example 4c). This is no ordinary "lyrical second theme". The texture and register suggest a chorale, maybe even an inward-turning prayer.

Example 4c. Op. 47, 1st mvt. (Exposition, mm. 87–116).

The melody of the new basic idea is nothing more than a very broad turn, repeated—on two levels, no less—and then ever so beautifully extended via diminution to a half cadence. It transforms the G#–A motive into something ineffably tender and contemplative, while also recalling the character and tempo of the Adagio introduction. In the recapitulation this recollection will be all the more overt: here within the exposition the key is the proto-Schubertian *major dominant* (see Schubert's Piano Sonata in A Minor, D. 784); in the recapitulation it will become the home-tonic major, thus reminding us that Beethoven opened his introduction in that major key but then took a distinctly non-Classical direction into his Presto, from major into minor. When the pianist returns to the minor dominant at bar 107, a plaintive, rueful dialogue begins—an interplay that seems profoundly intimate. Perhaps it should come as no surprise that, at the Adagio in bars 115–16, both players appear to have become lost in mutual thought, so much so that no cadence emerges to close this theme.

What follows at the Tempo I (Example 4d) is so clearly a return to the aggressive momentum of the transition materials that some writers hear that passage as having been *interrupted* at bar 90.[27]

Example 4d. Op. 47, 1st mvt. (Exposition, mm. 117–132).

---

27. See, for instance, Reti, *Thematic Patterns*, 153.

For example, Lawrence Kramer at first describes the chorale-like passage as "merely a parenthesis"; then he listens again and recognizes that "a parenthesis, too, can make a difference..."[28] If we take seriously the observation by theorists of form that secondary themes within Classical sonata-form movements close with authentic cadences, then a "new theme" does not begin at bar 117, because the preceding theme has not yet closed. I dare to propose that the explosive passage beginning at bar 117 might be heard as yet another huge continuation, one that balances an equally huge presentation—the violinist's tender sixteen-bar chorale as a CBI and the pianist's soulful, ten-bar varied repetition. In other words, like the main theme and like the transition, this first secondary theme takes on the structure, if not the character, of a sentence, to be concluded only with the tumultuous cadence at bar 144. But perhaps the sheer length of this process, not to mention the extreme contrast of its two parts, rules against such a view. At the least, it can be said that the octave leaps in both instruments within the continuation have been prepared by the violinist within the presentation, thus creating one motivic link—one small element of continuity. However one might choose to characterize the formal function of this passage, we can note that it drives to its cadence as if hell-bent upon reaching the fundamental, culminating theme of the exposition—the second secondary theme (ST²).

Here, for the first and only time, the pianist takes the lead (Example 4e). Epitomizing their role as carriers of the short-long rhythm, semitones as neighbours or passing tones now give the pianist the means by which to make an exultant ascent through an entire octave span. Then turns, borrowed from ST¹, allow for a slower descent from scale-degree $\hat{8}$ to $\hat{5}$, at which point this exceptionally short theme reaches its cadence and is snatched by up the violin. A canonic imitation between the violin and the piano's bass line intensifies the repetition, and then evaded cadences twice extend the theme by motivating "one more time" repetitions of its

---

28. Lawrence Kramer, *After the Lovedeath: Sexual Violence and the Making of Culture* (Berkeley: University of California Press, 1997), 82, 215. Kramer regards the "second theme" at bars 91–116 as one that defers the continuation of the "first theme". In short, he does not note that the "first theme" has closed in bar 45.

Example 4e. Op. 47, 1st mvt. (Exposition, mm. 140–79).

cadential idea.[29] The cadence finally achieved at bar 176 hardly seems like a goal, because the codettas that follow are unrelenting in the intensity with which they revive the transition's basic idea. The pianist's crashing chords urge the violinist to *slow down*, but when the violinist finally relinquishes quavers for whole semibreves and a fermata, one has the impression that this has happened purely out of exhaustion—from those extremely difficult bowings needed right up until the end.

To summarize, I portray the exposition of this movement as one in which two comrades, both virtuosi, collaborate but also challenge one another, within a dialogue that may be one of the most intensive demonstrations in the Classical repertoire of what can happen when composers and performers "perform" their fundamental interdependency. Like these two protagonists, but not in any way as if "assigned" to one or the other, two pitch-specific dyads collaborate to create a remarkable motivic network—one that spans across enormously contrasting themes of unprecedented length. Let me now draw attention to details within Beethoven's development section and his coda that surface as further manifestations of the motivic, formal, and technical ideas proposed as central thus far.

The development begins by underscoring the preeminent role of the semitone E–F; like the exposition, it opens with that specific motive in its original register. Here, however, the F-natural itself becomes the local tonic: the pianist introduces a quiet, major-mode version of ST^2 in that key. Apparently, neither instrument finds comfort in this gentler version of the theme; already by bar 200 the pianist is ready to abandon F major and hand the eight-bar phrase over to the violinist, who repeats it sequentially in G minor. A second sequence of the phrase begins in E-flat at bar 210, becomes fragmented, and results in some of the most brutally dissonant imitative counterpoint one can find in Beethoven's œuvre. As can be ascertained by examining the violin part from bar 214 onward, the pretence here is a straightforward descending-5ths sequence, but the pianist's raucous octaves all but annihilate the logic of that progression. The best one

---

29. See Janet Schmalfeldt, "Cadential Processes: The Evaded Cadence and the 'One More Time' Technique", *Journal of Musicological Research* 12 (1992): 1–52.

Example 4f. Op. 47, 1st mvt. (end of Development, mm. 310–344).

can do is note that the goal of this fracas is the dominant of the key with which the development began—F, but now F minor.

Within the terrifying passage in broken 3rds and 6ths that the pianist now faces, F minor again serves as an anchor (at bar 246), and then, after one last statement of ST² in D-flat (at bars 258–69), as the point of departure (at bar 270) for the retransition, which reaches the home dominant at bar 300. Within the ensuing dominant prolongation, the neighbour-motion E–F–E again takes centre stage in both parts; the pianist's cadenza even absorbs the F-natural within the dominant-9th chord, beginning at bar 308 (Example 4f, bar 310). But now the G#–A dyad must have its turn! And Beethoven can gain this in the pianist's part (see bars 313–15) by giving the violinist a sequential repetition of the pianist's cadenza, now prolonging the dominant of the subdominant (iv)—that is, the dominant of the very harmony with which the exposition eccentrically began. The violinist's sequence in turn motivates a "false recapitulation", a fully-fledged statement (at bars 325–35) of the main theme's first phrase, but now in D minor; this is of course the "wrong" key for a conventional recapitulation, but the *right* key, the subdominant, for a false-recapitulation effect in this movement. A great advantage of this manoeuvre is that it lands the phrase on an F-major chord at bar 334—one more opportunity to reinforce the role of F-natural as a pivotal tone in this movement. The semitone with which the false recapitulation began—A–B♭—now serves (at bars 336–40) as the impetus for the move towards the true home-key recapitulation; but note that the chord on F (at bars 340–43) plays the penultimate role in this modulation.

Now to Beethoven's coda, with excerpts shown at Examples 4g and 4h. The bridge into this section, with its move (at bars 513–16) into the key of the Neapolitan (flat-II = B♭), seems to have been motivated by the point just before the true recapitulation, in which the semitone A–B♭ played the pivotal role. This is the calm before the final storm. As the neighbour motion F–E insinuates itself in the pianist's bass (at bars 527–32), we approach the beginning of the main theme for its last appearance. This time the theme does what it has perhaps been longing to do for some time now: here the original stepwise ascent through the seventh will be expanded over the range of an entire octave plus seventh (Example 4g). The double-neighbour motion <E–F–D–E> (at bars 545–46) brings the ascent to a halt, and then the climax of the complete movement begins.

Beethoven tends to simplify his essential ideas in his codas, and this movement provides a case in point. Here the coda's climactic

Example 4g. Op. 47, 1st mvt. (Coda, mm. 532–66).

statement, beginning at bar 547, and given a "one more time" repetition at bar 553, features a segment of the original ascent in retrograde, now providing the fundamental *Urlinie* descent for the movement as a whole. There then follows a simplification of both the ascent and the *Urlinie* descent: each is reduced to a mere tonic arpeggiation, first up, then down. Finally, for a movement whose Adagio introduction has inspired not only an Adagio moment with fermata in the first secondary theme (in both the exposition and the recapitulation) but also nine additional fermatas, two last Adagios with fermatas seem required (Example 4h). The violinist's Adagio, at bars 575–78, gives the E–F motive one final major-mode setting; this statement seems to be hopeful—wistful for a positive outcome.

Example 4h. Op. 47, 1st mvt. (Coda, mm. 575–99).

The pianist's Adagio dashes the violinist's hope. Here the minor-mode plagal progression (iv–i)—so rich with the memory of the opening of the Presto, and so redolent of the lament tradition with which it is associated—would seem to express something beyond sorrow, something so deeply personal that it cannot be put into words. From this perspective, the gruff, furioso conclusion at the Tempo I becomes a heroic effort to put away such dark thoughts. The movement cannot, however, escape its two motivic semitones: they pervade the music all the way into the pianist's final G#–A.

One certainly cannot claim that the technique of creating inter-textual motivic connections was new for Beethoven in 1803.[30] But from the first to the second movement of Op. 47, his increasing concern for a motivically cyclic approach to composition could not be more palpable. As shown in Example 5a, Beethoven's second movement, in F major, features a theme for variations in which the first phrase begins with F–E and the second with G#–A. Relative to the Presto, the direction of each of the two semitones has been reversed. Especially salient are the materials of the B-section within this theme as rounded binary (Example 5b): the cadential progression in the dominant at bars 21–22 highlights the E–F motion, with F-natural now as an incomplete neighbour; then, twice within the standing-on-the-dominant phrase, the pianist labours upward by step to the E

Example 5a. Op. 47, 2nd mvt. (mm. 1–8).

---

30. From within Beethoven's piano sonatas, for example, the rolled B-flat chord at the beginning of the slow movement of the "Tempest" Sonata unequivocally recalls the rolled chord with which the first movement begins (as well as the other rolled chords within that movement—at bar 7, at the beginning of the development section, and within the recapitulation). The opening stepwise descent in D major from $\hat{5}$ to the octave below at the beginning of the "Pastorale" Piano Sonata, Op. 28 (1801), looks forward to the simpler, shorter descent, now fundamentally from $\hat{5}$ to $\hat{1}$, within the initial basic idea of the finale. This relatively strong connection might retrospectively give substance to the idea that the fleeting stepwise $\hat{5}$ to $\hat{1}$ descent at the beginning of the Andante, in D minor, relates to the openings of both the first and last movements in Op. 28.

Example 5b. Op. 47, 2nd mvt. (mm. 17–28).

and embellishes it again with the F. In case we have missed the point
—hardly likely by now—the phrase concludes with a fragmentation
that yields two more *sforzando*-accented F-naturals.

It is now well known that the finale of Op. 47 was originally
meant to serve as the last movement of Beethoven's earlier A-major
Violin Sonata, Op. 30, No. 1 (1802). Scholars and performers alike
agree that Beethoven's decision to transfer this finale to Op. 47 was
wise, as was his last-minute addition of a big, loud A-major chord
in the piano at the beginning of the movement, clearly a reference
to the pianist's initial harmony within the first movement's introduction (Example 6a). After that chord, the pianist's very first interval is G#–A. But the pianist's voice is only a counterpoint to the violinist's soprano here; and given that this movement is in A *major,*
analysts will search in vain for the counterpart semitone, E–F-*natural.*
On the other hand, the *idea* of the semitone within a short-long
rhythm—materializing wherever it can be realised—unquestionably
rests at the basis of this marvellous movement. Just as notable as the
pervasiveness of semitones is the undeniable connection, observed
by Réti, between the first secondary theme (ST[1]) of the finale
(Example 6b) and the second secondary theme (ST[2]) of the first

Example 6a. Op. 47, Finale (mm. 1–8).

Example 6b. Op. 47, Finale (mm. 60–70).

movement (at bars 144–56).[31] If, in the first movement, that theme stormed its way upward through the octave, in the finale the octave ascent, followed again by the slower descent from $\hat{8}$ to $\hat{5}$, embraces the jaunty, tarantella character of the movement as a whole, as if to brush away the memory of the earlier turmoil.

* * *

31. Reti, *Thematic Patterns*, 158–59.

Leo Tolstoy may have contributed the single most provocative focal point in the reception history of Beethoven's Op. 47. I refer to his famous novella, *The Kreutzer Sonata*, from 1889, and to recent musicological efforts to interpret this work in respect of the role that music has played in the construction of gender relations. Tolstoy probably knew nothing about George Bridgetower's role in the première of the sonata, but it seems clear that he recognized in this piece what Lawrence Kramer has described as "its explosive incongruity", its "importation of formal monumentality and emotional ferocity" into a medium that hitherto, and even long thereafter, was associated with the salon.[32] Thus, when the protagonist of the story, in the thick of a disastrous marriage, introduces his wife to a violinist, arranges for her as amateur pianist to rehearse privately with him, and finally witnesses their semi-public performance of Op. 47, he senses that a social boundary has been mightily crossed; the performance itself serves as the catalyst for the husband's jealousy and his brutal murder of the wife.

Speaking about the first movement of Op. 47, Tolstoy's protagonist asks: "Do you know the first movement, its presto? You do? … Ah! It is a fearful thing, that sonata. Especially that movement. And in general music's a fearful thing! What is it? I don't know …What does it do? And why does it do to us what it does? They say music exalts the soul. Nonsense, it is not true! … It has neither an exalting nor a debasing effect but an agitating one.... Music makes me forget myself, my real position; it transports me to some other position not my own." And, a little later, he says: "Take that Kreutzer Sonata for instance, how can that first presto be played in a drawing-room among ladies in low-necked dresses? To hear that played, to clap a little, and then to eat ices and talk of the latest scandal?"[33]

For me as pianist, a most amazing detail about Tolstoy's novella is that he portrays the wife as having been able to work up a performance

---

32. Kramer, *After the Lovedeath*, 41.

33. Leo Tolstoy, *The Kreutzer Sonata and Other Stories*, trans. David McDuff (Harmondsworth: Penguin Books, 1985), 96–98; and Tolstoy, *The Kreutzer Sonata and Other Stories*, trans. Louise and Aylmer Maude and J. D. Duff (Oxford: Oxford University Press, 1997), 144,145.

of Beethoven's "Kreutzer" over the span of roughly one week! But it goes without saying that the character of the "Kreutzer" plays the greater role in the story than its technical difficulties. For Kramer, what the husband hears in the first movement, "what he has turned procurer in order to hear it, is a movement of transcendence, a breaking-through into a spirituality quite inconsistent with the lust, décolletage, and triviality of the drawing room".[34] Both Kramer and, before him, Richard Leppert stress that not only is Beethoven's first movement "not salon music: it is not music of and for women. It is fundamentally masculine, even phallic, in character as Beethoven's music can be... The feminine is erased from the score. [The] wife and her partner both take on the sonoric roles of men, a violation scripted by Beethoven that [the husband] cannot tolerate".[35] Finally, Kramer reminds us that "for many years it was considered indecent for women to play [the violin]";[36] this was certainly the case in 1803. And yet, neither Kramer nor Leppert considers the specific male violinist who premièred Op. 47. Nor, by the way, does Bridgetower make an appearance in Jander's or Réti's analysis; for that matter, he becomes a mere footnote or one-liner, if not utterly disappears, in the commentary about Op. 47 by such preeminent Beethoven historians as Maynard Solomon, William Kinderman, and Lewis Lockwood.

Since Beethoven most surely did not compose Op. 47 with a female violinist in mind, and if his writing in the first movement —especially the continuous string-crossing idea at the beginning of his transition, which pervades the movement—was inspired by violinistic technique, then perhaps it should not be at all surprising that the Presto of Op. 47 has been interpreted as "masculine".

---

34. Kramer, *After the Lovedeath*, 79.
35. Richard Leppert, *The Sight of Sound: Music, Representation, and the History of the Body* (Berkeley: University of California Press, 1993), 176.
36. Kramer, *After the Lovedeath*, 238. An exception is the case of Regina Strinasacchi (1761–1829), the brilliant and famous young Mantuan violinist for whom Mozart composed his Violin Sonata in B-flat, K. 454, and with whom he premièred that work at the Kärntnertortheater in the presence of Emperor Joseph II on 28 April 1784. I am grateful to several colleagues, and in particular to Elaine Sisman, for alerting me to the phenomenon of Strinasacchi.

This outlook does not, of course, explain the many differences in character between Op. 47 and the other nine sonatas for violin that Beethoven produced—none of them presumably with women violinists in mind. In short, perhaps Beethoven really did write the first movement of this piece "with Bridgetower in mind".

Reports have it that Beethoven and Bridgetower were constant companions during the month of May 1803, when Bridgetower was in Vienna; two short letters from Beethoven to Bridgetower during that month—whether before or after their performance together (the dates do not clarify)—attest to their intimacy.[37] More pertinent, a manuscript of the exposition of the first movement discovered in 1965 confirms that Beethoven originally dedicated his Op. 47 to Bridgetower, as follows: "Sonata mulattica Composta per il Mulatto Brischdauer / gran passo e compositore mulattico" ("mulatto sonata composed for the mulatto Bridgetower, great loon and mulatto composer").[38] However it might be translated, I take "gran passo" as jocular and deeply affectionate.

The story also goes that the composer's and violinist's friendship broke up "over a girl"[39]—possibly because Bridgetower made a snide remark about a woman of whom Beethoven was fond. We will undoubtedly never know what really happened; but a letter from Ries to publisher Nikolaus Simrock of 22 October 1803 indicates that already by then, Beethoven had decided to dedicate the Op. 47 sonata to the renowned Parisian violinist Rodolphe Kreutzer and to Louis Adam, the foremost pianist in Paris at the time. Why? Here we have an explanation, and it smacks of unabashed opportunism. Beethoven's dissatisfaction with his freelance life in Vienna had led him to threaten a move to Paris; his *Eroica* Symphony, carrying the dedication to Napoleon until May 1804, his Op. 47, and probably even his newly begun opera *Léonore* (based on J. N. Bouilly's French libretto) were all to have paved the way for a smooth entrée into Parisian musical life.[40] The

---

37. See Beethoven, *The Letters of Beethoven*, Nos. 74 and 75 (91–92).
38. See Brandenburg, "Zur Textgeschichte," 114.
39. Thayer, *Thayer's Life of Beethoven*, 333.
40. See Solomon, *Beethoven*, 169–70.

great irony here is that Kreutzer detested Beethoven's works and refused ever to perform Op. 47. As for Bridgetower, after around 1848 he seems to have slipped into obscurity. He died in a back street of London in 1860; his death certificate is signed with an X by an illiterate woman.

On a brighter note, let us applaud the fact that stereotypes of the past about music as gendered "masculine", or "feminine", are now being critically examined and contextualized, and that they are for the most part avoided today. Now, one can hear recorded performances of Op. 47 by, for example, Martha Argerich and Gidon Kremer, Clara Haskil and Arthur Grumiaux, Lambert Orkis and Anne-Sophie Mutter, and, especially touching, Claude Frank and his daughter, Pamela. Whatever the gender combination, performers of Op. 47 would, I think, all agree that this piece cries out for an extraordinary synergy—a genuine coming together of soulmates in music. Bridgetower himself felt that the "Kreutzer" Sonata should have been the "Bridgetower" Sonata. Let us take this opportunity to bestow upon him what should most probably have been his fortune.

INTIMACY AND IMPERSONALITY IN LATE BEETHOVEN: CONTRAST AND THE STAGING OF SUBJECTIVITY*

Scott Burnham

One of the chapters dealing with the late quartets in Joseph Kerman's still vital 1966 book *The Beethoven Quartets* carries the title "Voice". The term can cover a range of phenomena, from what Kerman calls the "sheer songfulness" of the late quartets to strikingly staged incursions of a vocal "human element" into the landscape of much of Beethoven's late-period instrumental music. These latter include such passages as the *Arioso dolente* of the *Piano Sonata in A-flat, Op. 110,* or the melodramatic recitative in the March movement of the *String Quartet in A minor, Op. 132.* In the context of instrumental music, the simulation of voice and song can be heard as a move toward greater intimacy and vulnerability.

Another one of Kerman's chapters is entitled "Contrast". A drastic strand of contrast in Beethoven's late style is that which obtains between moments of staged subjectivity and other musics that evoke machines, or that sound so monumental as to seem to transcend the human. What does it mean to contrast these realms, to question the human with the superhuman or with the non-human?

A powerful 20th-century interpretation of such staggering contrast holds that Beethoven created the conditions for a *coincidentia oppositorum,* opposites brought together in a mystic vision radiating from some central experience (J.W.N. Sullivan), or, at least, that he promoted a sense of unity in diversity or *multum in parvo*.[1] The primary analytical mandate stemming from this belief has been the search for ways to unite the disparate shards of

---

* This essay was inspired by some remarks made by my colleague and friend J. K. Randall about fifteen years ago, on the nature of contrast in *Op. 130.*

1. J.W.N. Sullivan, *Beethoven: His Spiritual Development* (New York: Vintage Books, 1960, orig. 1927), passim; Martin Cooper, *Beethoven: The Last Decade 1817–1827* (London: Oxford University Press, *1970*), 420.

human reality heard in the late music. Pitch proves, time and again, to be the most dependable agent of coherence in this effort, especially when its agency is concealed to some degree—thus Carl Dahlhaus speaks of a subthematic realm, and Deryck Cooke (in the *ne plus ultra* of such approaches) seeks to demonstrate the Unity of all five Late Quartets in an abstract four-note figure (now that's very *parvus*, and think of the *multum* that results!).[2] Another, rather different, tradition dates from Theodor Adorno's engagement with the late style.[3] For writers operating within this tradition, the contrasts in Beethoven's late works are heard to be the means of a critique of the composer's earlier style, or perhaps of music itself, or, more recently, of our own analytical methods. These latter approaches do not attempt to analyze away the apparent discontinuities of this music in the name of underlying unity, but instead hear the disjunctions as offering a distinctly different kind of critical payoff, as in Adorno's sense of the late style as the sound of the subject absenting itself, or Daniel Chua's sense of the *String Quartet in B-flat, Op. 130* as profiling the "impossibility of closure", that most Beethovenian of musical values.[4]

But in thus attempting to *enlist* the contrasts, either in the Modernist act of finding an underlying, secret, and abstract common denominator that redeems unity or in the Postmodernist act of considering the ubiquity of contrast and disparity as a critique—or even repudiation—of unity, perhaps we are letting our anxiety about wholeness and closure dictate the terms of the experience. In doing so, we may lose sight of the nature of these contrasts. Why *these* contrasts?

One way to take in these contrasts is as a potent form of so-called Romantic irony. In Romantic irony, the artist (usually a writer) creates an illusion of beauty and suddenly destroys it with a drastic change of tone, or a personal intrusion. Rey Longyear

---

2. Carl Dahlhaus, *Ludwig van Beethoven: Approaches to his Music*, trans. Mary Whittall (Oxford: Clarendon Press, 1991), Chapter 12, "Subthematicism"; Deryck Cooke, "The Unity of Beethoven's Late Quartets", *Music Review* 24 (1963): 30–49.
3. Adorno, "Spätstil Beethovens", in *Moments Musiquax: Neu gedrückte Aufsätze 1928–1962* (Frankfurt am Main: Suhrkamp Verlag, 1964).
4. Daniel K. L. Chua, *The "Galitzin" Quartets of Beethoven: Opp. 127 132, 130* (Princeton: Princeton University Press, 1995), 244.

wrote an essay in 1970 entitled "Beethoven and Romantic Irony", in which he pointed out Beethoven's tendency in the late style to juxtapose extreme human registers, to stage contrasts between the exalted and the vulgar, sublime and grotesque.[5] Longyear cites such junctures as the shift in the *Ninth Symphony* finale from the exalted setting of the words "und der Cherub steht vor Gott" to the street march in Turkish style, with bass drum and triangle, or the shift in the *A minor String Quartet* from the ethereal solemnity of the ending of the *Heiliger Dankgesang* movement to the choppy bluster of the opening of the March movement.

In both these examples, Beethoven seems to be wrestling with the problem of the presence of the transcendent, or the divine, within the human realm: boundaries between divine and human, or ideal and real, are rudely drawn and enforced. Beethoven's large-scale, public works of this period, the *Missa Solemnis* and the *Ninth Symphony*, can be said to make this problem their own, and gaping musical contrasts lie at the heart of their engagement with it.

The *Missa Solemnis* juxtaposes the monumental and the personal throughout. Consider the opening utterance of the entire Mass, on the word "Kyrie" (O Lord). Massed choral sound gives way to the sound of vocal soloists, as we hear two different ways of addressing the Deity: the chorus provides a grandiose, monolithic call to the Lord, on single harmonies; the soloists inject a more human note of pleading or obeisance with lines that consist of an expressive descending interval.

The Mass text of course abounds in references to the Deity. In some notable cases, Beethoven sets these references with a sudden influx of monumental scoring. One such string of references occurs in the Gloria, bars 176–190, in the appositional series of descriptors "Domine Deus, Rex coelestis, Pater omnipotens" (Lord God, King of the heavens, all-powerful Father). In the final pairing of this series, the juxtaposition of the human term "father" and the epithet "omnipotens" sharpens the sense of the Deity: no longer a distant lord or king, the Deity is now a father—but an all-powerful Father. This brings power up close, in the person of a family member. To

5. Rey M. Longyear, "Beethoven and Romantic Irony", in *The Creative World of Beethoven*, ed. Paul Henry Lang (New York: Norton, 1970), 145–62.

convey this awesome propinquity of all-power, the trombones enter for the first time in the Mass on the word "omnipotens", where they reinforce a striking harmony of great duration that projects sublime otherness. Then the human element materializes once again: immediately after the sheer sonic force of "omnipotens", the music becomes more intimately scaled, as the text appeals to the Son of God with the words "domine fili unigenite, Jesu Christe".

Later in the Gloria, bars 269–275, the phrase "qui sedes ad dexteram patris" (who sits on the right of the father) is followed by "miserere nobis" (have mercy on us). As the music approaches the pater, the volume goes up, and we hear a big fanfare on B-flat major, with dotted rhythms and rapidly repeated notes in the strings. And then, at "miserere nobis", the music drops from the V of B-flat to D-flat, pianissimo, with fragmented repeated notes. The shift of subjective register could hardly be more palpable, in dynamics, rhythm, melody and harmony (root motion down a major third became a common way to project a shift between two different subjective realms—a common tone is held while the ground seems to change under one's feet).

Sometimes the contrast occurs between the representation of a congregation within a vast cathedral space and the individual worshipper. The end of the Credo seems to traverse the very vaults of the cathedral, first with a resounding series of Amens and then with a kind of super-plagal cadence which comes on like a suffusion of grace emanating from overhead and settling upon the multitude below (bars 463–472). And then, as the Sanctus opens, the scene seems to move from the public space of an imposing cathedral to the personal space of the individual, kneeling before the altar (to invoke Tovey's image for the outset of the Sanctus).[6]

The *Ninth Symphony* can also be heard to stage an encounter between humans and the Deity, or, to speak more broadly, between the ideal and the real. The Ode to Joy theme itself acts as a resonant fusion of human and superhuman, individual and congregation: the tune works both as a quiet singular voice and as a roaring choral statement, as an utterance that can be both intimate

6. Donald Francis Tovey, *Essays in Music Analysis, Volume V: Choral Music* (London: Oxford University Press, 1937), 179.

and monumental. But if the Ode to Joy theme can be heard as a hopeful song of fusion, another story about the relation of human and divine can be heard to surge throughout the symphony. This story is driven at first by violent contrasts and then by a kind of accommodating détente between the two realms, in which the starry heavens serve to indicate the adjusted relation of the Deity to humankind (this would make the *Ninth* into a kind of theodicy, or an attempt to "justify the ways of God to man"). I once fashioned this narrative as a kind of "pitch story", namely the story of B-flat—because this pitch speaks across the contrasts; it is present at each crucial scene.[7]

The first movement of the *Ninth Symphony* presents glimpses of B-flat as an alternative key centre, and the pitch is crucial for an electric moment of elision at the outset of the recapitulation (bars 313–314). In the slow movement, we get to live in B-flat as if in some sort of serene, ideal realm. But remember how Beethoven tears us away from this realm, with the raucous *Schreckensfanfare* at the outset of the finale. In this famously dissonant opening, the pitch A directly confronts the B-flat triad, shredding its implied serenity with sudden horror—as if to say, or rather to scream, that we cannot reside in such an idealized space. And we are soon to experience another direct contrast of the pitches B-flat and A. At the text "the cherub stands before God" we hear a strongly tonicized A. Then the bass drops to F (again the drop of a major third!), which has the effect of transforming the A from a grounded root into a radiant third, like a beam of light. But apparently we cannot face the direct light of God. Instead the sound drops an almost unimaginable distance, to the lowest note of the contrabassoon, a croaking B-flat at the bottom of the orchestra, as the scene changes to a Turkish-style street march.

Again we are turned rudely away from the ideal. If in the first stage of this process the pitch A rips us from the paradisal, ideal realm of B-flat, this second stage elevates the pitch A to the sacred throne of the Deity, while transforming the key of B-flat into a

7. Burnham, "How Music Matters: Poetic Content Revisited", in Nicholas Cook and Mark Everist, eds. *Rethinking Music* (Oxford: Oxford University Press, 1999), 208–212.

realm here below. A was real, but is now ideal; B-flat was ideal, but is now real. Nor is this simple reversal of fortune the final move, bracing as it is. We do not remain barred from the ideal. The music will find a way to get these pitches to co-exist, to accommodate this contrast.

A dialectical resolution of the A and B-flat can be said to occur in the middle section of the finale. Beethoven stages an epiphany here. Shortly after the words "Ahnest du den Schöpfer, Welt" the scene broadens to include a musical representation of the stars above: "Über Sternen muß er wohnen". Here the B-flat is placed high and away from the A, as a twinkling dissonance, a minor ninth within the structural dominant of the entire movement, the dominant that triggers the large-scale return of D major (which combines the Ode to Joy theme from the first section of the finale with the theme from the middle section). With the appearance of the *Sternenzelt*, the starry canopy, the contrast between divine and human is mediated at the tonal fulcrum of the last movement. Just as we cannot look directly into the sun but can look into distant suns, so we can face the light of God not directly but through the constructed mediation of the stars, impossibly remote yet always available. But Beethoven's stars also provide a potentially double-edged experience: are they the twinkling benevolence of reassuring presence or the sign of absolute impersonality, or even absolute absence? Remember Pascal's complaint: "Le silence éternel de ces espaces infinies m'effraie".[8]

The *Ninth Symphony* does not close with this vision of the starry heavens above. Instead, the percussion battery from the Turkish march (bass drum, triangle, cymbal) returns at the very end, giving the orchestra something like the sound of a mechanical calliope. In other words, a musical machine gets the last word.[9] This complicates the situation in a fascinating way, tempting one to recalibrate the perhaps too-facile interpretation of a dialectical

---

8. Cf. Nicholas Cook on this passage: "…here the music is the very embodiment of cosmic emptiness." *Beethoven, Symphony No. 9*, Cambridge Music Handbooks (Cambridge: Cambridge University Press, 1993), 104.
9. Not all conductors choose to bring this aspect out. Mahler and others actually reduced the percussion at the ending, perhaps thinking it unseemly. For a modern-day recording that does not stint on the drums, try Roger Norrington.

negotiation of ideal and real. For what does it mean to follow the newly-empowered subjectivity achieved through the finale's grand dialectic with this kind of music? To hear a juxtaposition of human and machine at the end of the *Ninth Symphony* is to hear the music ask a different question altogether, one that would seem to engage subjectivity at a more constitutive level. We may now turn to some of Beethoven's other late-style music, which can be heard to put such a question to us even more sharply.

* * *

If, in the *Missa Solemnis* and the *Ninth Symphony,* human subject-ivity is dramatically contrasted with a perceived transcendence, and various mediations and accommodations are staged, how do such contrasts play out in Beethoven's late chamber music? Here the contrasts seem to float free of a religious or spiritual context into other *mises en scène* that can be even more provocative, more unsettling. Among the many fabled disjunctions in the late quartets, I will focus on those of the *String Quartet in B-flat, Op. 130.* For this work, above all, consistently translates into a different register the

Example 1 Op. 130, final six bars of Cavatina, opening theme of Grosse Fuge *(bars 1–10).*

contrast between human and other found in the Mass and the *Ninth Symphony*. Here the intimacy is more vulnerable, the impersonal more mechanical—the contrast is profiled, hard to ignore, less grounded in some ready-to-hand dramatic narrative.

To begin, we need something demonstrably human. We have long honoured the Cavatina as perhaps the single most emotional movement in all of Beethoven. The biographical dimension seems to confirm this, for Beethoven himself apparently claimed (to Karl Holz) that he wept when he composed this movement.[10] The contrast between the very end of the Cavatina and the opening of the *Grosse Fuge* could hardly be more pronounced—from the impossibly vulnerable to the impassively invulnerable.

The pitch G, as a shared feature, profiles the transformation. At the end of the Cavatina, the G is caressed by a dissonant passing tone, left exposed on top of the final harmony as well as doubled within. This octave doubling of the G subtly prepares for what is to come, but its more immediate effect is to add a stripe of colour outside the warm, closely spaced E-flat major triad in the lower strings, as if to paint on the outside of a window that which is already felt to be glowing within, or, shifting the metaphor to a cliché, as if to wear its heart on the sleeve. And then the G's hyper-human, expressive vulnerability finds its mechanical opposite on the other side of the Cavatina's double bar line: with the amplification of the G into those loud octaves at the outset of the *Grosse Fuge*, the pitch becomes a kind of Frankenstein, shocked into twitchy mechanical life.[11]

And it isn't just the *Grosse Fuge* that creates such contrast: Beethoven's later, alternative finale also begins with the pitch G, now configured as mechanical, spinning-wheel octaves (the exact pitches are deftly extracted from the oddly voiced final chord of the Cavatina).

---

10. See Daniel Chua's brilliant reading of this reputed act of weeping, and what it implies about bourgeois interiority. Chua, 196.
11. Cf. Richard Kramer on the opening G of the *Grosse Fuge*, "Wrenched from the pathos of the Cavatina, its graceless grace notes wrest the two middle-register Gs from that famous simultaneity with which the Cavatina expires and inflate them to an expanse of four octaves…This opening G stands apart". In "Between Cavatina and Ouverture: Opus 130 and the Voices of Narrative", *Beethoven Forum* 1 (1992), 178.

Example 2. Op. 130, bars 1–10 of Finale. Allegro (alternate finale).

This creates a quite different effect but with no less of a contrast. For a pantomimic image of this contrast, imagine the G at the end of the Cavatina as a Chaplinesque figure placing his hands on his heart in a scene of touching pathos, slowly opening them back out toward you, and then—with the bouncing octaves of the new finale—beginning to juggle with them: the hands of the emoting human empathizer become those of the mechanically entertaining performer.

Next consider the move into the Cavatina from the preceding G-major movement designated as a Danza alla tedesca. This movement sounds like the product of a mechanical "squeeze box". And toward the end of the dance, the machine breaks down into inert fragments, only to spring back to "life" for a final peroration.

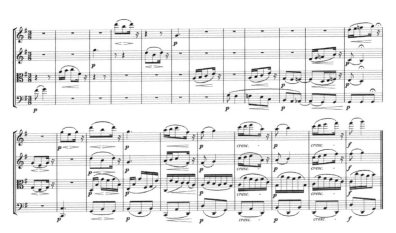

Example 3. Op. 130, Danza alla tedesca, bars 129 to end.

Thus the emotional Cavatina is framed at either end by these more distinctly mechanical musics. And of course it frames its own most emotional moment, namely, the famous "beklemmt" passage that forms its middle section. The result of all this is a multiply-layered framing of writhingly emotive music.

And more contrasts await. Recall the effect of moving from the D-flat Andante movement into the Danza alla tedesca. Here we step from a "lyric scherzo…of unparalleled charm and eloquence" (Charles Rosen)[12] into the short-winded *Knittelvers* ethos of the German dance. Beethoven also distances the movements tonally, with the disjunction of a tritone between D-flat and G. The establishment of the key of G begins a gradual preoccupation with G, which will morph from comic tonic to burnished third (Cavatina) to fraught sixth scale degree (both finales).

Even within the Andante movement itself, the very seat of graceful lyricism, mechanical moments obtrude, putting the temporal flow of song on pause. Near the outset, a pizzicato extension to the theme presents a material contrast by means of the now detached motive from the end of the theme.

Example 4. Andante, Op. 130, bars 8–10, end of theme and pizzicato extension.

This contrast is sharpened toward the end of the movement, where the pizzicato material becomes as if a mechanized clockwork:

And a little way after this passage, the piece gets stuck once again, now on a dotted motive:

---

12. Rosen, *The Classical Style*, 511.

Example 5. Andante, Op. 130, bars 66–70, Tempo I.

Example 6. Andante, Op. 130, bars 79 to first beat of 85.

Contrasts between lyric impulse and mechanical succession occur in the opening movement as well. The songful second theme is approached mechanistically, with a chromatic line that marches in rhythm from F up to D-flat. This is followed by an expressive and leisurely descent through the G-flat major triad in the cello that then grounds the lyrical leap and steps of the violin's theme:

Example 7. Adagio/Allegro, Op. 130, bars 51–57.

At the point of its cadence, this theme devolves into mechanical semiquavers, sped up reiterations of its descending steps. Once again, a lyrical motive gets detached and "mechanized."

Example 8. Adagio/Allegro, Op. 130, bars 63–70.

In fact, contrast is the mainspring of this movement, one of the first things we know about it. The opening page of the quartet presents two different scenes in close succession—they entail two distinctive kinds of subjective experience. The first of these begins with voices that descend together in semitones and then split off into harmonic progression, like a melancholy impulse branching out into the beginning of a thought process; the thinking continues with pensive imitation, pausing on a dominant seventh (bars 7–14). The scene then shifts radically, with an Allegro cascade of semiquavers surging over and around a prominent gesture of an ascending fourth. The usual locutionary force of this rising interval is oddly undercut by reversing the dynamics (we leap from forte to piano); this has a stunted quality that will be heard to relate to some moments later in the quartet.[13] Later we encounter these two musics at the beginning of the development section, now played as fragmentary, tonally disjunct vignettes:

Example 9. Op. 130, Allegro/Adagio, bars 94–101.

The final page of the movement returns once again to this foundational contrast, dovetailing the alternations: yearning semitones from the pensive adagio music reach directly into the allegro cascade.

Example 10. Op. 130, Allegro/Adagio, bars 214 (pickup into 214)–222.

---

13. My thanks to J. K. Randall, who brought this aspect of the rising fourth motive to my attention.

By this point, the contrast is itself thematic.

Jumping to the other end of the quartet, a closer look at the Overtura of the *Grosse Fuge* reveals that its contrasting takes on the opening line touch in short order on some of the different subjective registers we have been listening for: mechanical, humanized, stunted.[14]

Example 11. Op. 130, Grosse Fuge, bars 1–30 (Overtura).

The thrumming, high-voltage octaves of the first ten bars discharge into a "violent trill"[15] that lurches into sudden silence. Then the angular line whips by in "fast forward"; then silence; then again "fast forward", transposed (bars 11–16). These dis-

---

14. Martin Cooper underlines the adumbrating function of these "takes" when he describes the Overtura as a "cinematic trailer of coming events". Cooper, 382. Kerman emphasizes the visceral impact of the Overtura, saying that it "hurls all the thematic versions at the listener's head like a handful of rocks". Kerman, 277.
15. Kerman, ibid.

tinctly mechanical manipulations barely have time to register when a more humanized version steps forth, with ingratiating harmony and counterpoint (bars 17–25). The next and last utterance before the fugue proper is perhaps the most extraordinary of all: the first violin mouths a lobotomized version of the theme, gapped, stunted, drained of volition (bars 26–30).

With this last sound in our ears, we remember the stunted ascending fourth of the first movement's Allegro. These faltering "humanoid" utterances — as though simulating a voice under some sort of distorting stress — can also be aligned with the "beklemmt" first violin of the Cavatina. But whereas the "beklemmt" voice seems hyper-human, the sound of vulnerable emotion, the gapped violin line of the *Grosse Fuge* seems subhuman. And these different voicings can in turn be juxtaposed with the hyper-machine utterances no human voice could muster, such as appear at the outset of the *Grosse Fuge*'s Overtura. The Overtura can now be heard as a motion through a range of subjective registers, from supra-human to human to subhuman.

What are the available cultural referents for such contrastive voicings? These may be distinctly post-Kantian manoeuvres, testing the limits of subjectivity at both ends. Or perhaps it is more a forcing of the issue of subjectivity by contrasting human and machine, human and subhuman, human and divine. It is, of course, very Beethovenian to force the issue; even Schubert commented that Beethoven went "beyond good taste". By distinctly pushing *these* contrasts, making them central to the musical logic, to the musical experience, to musical presence — confronting the human with the impersonal, the inorganic, the mechanical — is Beethoven reminding us that music is itself mechanical, the result of machines, that music is itself an elegant simulacrum of subjectivity? He seems to be questioning his affective relation to music — our affective relation to music — for he can now stage the most human of states (as in the choked up Cavatina) and then sweep it away with the *Grosse Fuge*. Or he can stage a grandiose epiphany in the *Ninth Symphony*, and then let the work conclude with a mechanized orchestra. At any point in any movement, graceful music can get mechanically stuck, or mechanical music can become gracefully eloquent. Do these manoeuvres speak to a growing anxiety about the extent to which we, as humans, are machines; how even the act of giving voice is an instrumental act?[16] Is our very consciousness — so often projected onto music — at stake here? Is Beethoven transforming the human into "the human"? Is he putting scare quotes on the last aspect of our identity we would be willing to question?

Stepping back from these premature and melodramatic implications, a simple methodological message remains: we need not analyze away the contrasts in late Beethoven; nor must we perforce regard them only as contrasts, as disjunctions. Rather, we can begin to consider the extent to which we are hearing a fascinating way of staging subjectivity: modern, post-revolutionary, post-Kantian, always pushing at the extremes, unsentimental yet never hardened against hope, at once vulnerable and impassive, inclusive and idiosyncratic. Compounded of irony and paradox, Beethoven's late music somehow exercises both a more distanced critique *and* a more intimate sincerity, seeming to make the one a condition of the other.

What do we hear? Bitter fruit, belly laugh, whispered hope, nihilist's howl, dancing machine, singing heart, sublime wall of sound, last empty hallway.

In an age pervaded by stagings of subjectivity, from the humanly-scaled *Bildungsroman* to the all-consuming *Weltseele* of Hegelian idealism, Beethoven's late music may well be the most drastic staging of them all. Alexander Pope once characterized humankind as "the glory, jest, and riddle of the world".[17] Much great art of the modern age may be said to ratify this conceit. But Beethoven? He forces the issue.

---

16. The fascination with inorganic and mechanical simulations of life is a potent theme in German Romanticism, as in the tradition of stories having to do with mines and the supernatural, such as Ludwig Tieck's "Der Runenberg" or E.T.A. Hoffmann's "Das Bergwerk von Falun". (It even extends into the 20th century, as in the third chapter of Thomas Mann's *Doktor Faustus,* in which Adrian and Serenus explore heliotropic crystal formations at the behest of Adrian's father, who tearfully emphasizes their life-like qualities). Even more relevant, perhaps, is the invocation of musical automata in this same period, as in Hoffmann's story "Die Automate".

17. Alexander Pope, "Essay on Man: Epistle 2," line 18, in *Poetry and Prose of Alexander Pope*, ed. by Aubrey Williams (Boston: Houghton Mifflin, 1969), 131.

OF EPIGONES, AFTERMATHS, AND ACHIEVEMENT: THE HEINE SONGS OF FRANZ LACHNER

Susan Youens

Franz Schubert had company in his brief encounter with Heinrich Heine's poetry at some unknown time late in his short life: two other composers resident in Vienna who were friends of Schubert in the last years of his life, were also drawn to this poet's works. One was the Bavarian-born Franz Lachner (the other was Johann Vesque von Püttlingen, 1803–1883, whose ninety-plus Heine songs anticipate Hugo Wolf in certain aspects[1]). How Lachner (1803–1890) reacted to Schubert's influence after the great composer's death tells all sorts of tales about the attempts of those who come after genius to assert their own voices. That Lachner was acutely aware of Schubert's songs is encoded over and over again in his own; that he sought consciously to differentiate himself from Schubert is also apparent. In both exercises, he was also taking part in a great debate regarding the nature of song, a debate played out in the tens of thousands of songs flooding the market throughout the long nineteenth century. What was song, fundamentally? What was its proper sphere? What words could be set to music, in what way, to what audience? What should be the relationship between "poetry", its purposes also hotly debated, and music when the two were yoked together? What were the roles of song in shaping society, in moulding the hearts and minds of the consumers of *Lied*? What codes of conduct, what avenues of feeling, did these songs uphold, undermine, or bring into being? How many different things could "song" be? In the half-century between Schubert's death and Hermann Mendel's *Musikalisches Conversations-Lexikon* of 1876, song had become so multifarious that the exasperated encyclopaedist throws up his hands in despair at ever pinning it down. "To designate the true inner and outward

---

1. See the author's Heinrich *Heine and the Lied* (Cambridge 2007), pp. 142–173 for more about Vesque von Püttlingen's songs.

nature of a song is very difficult, in fact, almost impossible, especially given the very imprecise use of the word as the name for a
certain kind of poetic and musical style", the writer concludes, the writer concludes,
refusing to grapple further with the Hydra-headed beast of definition.[2] Heine's importance in music history has to do in considerable measure with his role in precipitating those works that made
song hard to define, and Schubert's brief rendezvous with him
sealed the deal. Schubert may have rejected Heine, but the six
masterpieces created before he returned to the poetic realm of
those who loved Goethe rather than Heine became the model of
modernity in song for a new generation of composers.

On 1 November 1881, the seventy-eight year old Bavarian composer Franz Lachner published his *Erinnerungen an Schubert und
Beethoven* in Vienna's *Die Presse*. Here, he writes of midday meals
at Leopold Haidvogel's inn with "a plump, round young man, of
less than medium height, with a high forehead, a pug-nose, curly
and thinning hair, rounded shoulders and hunched posture",
someone whose eyes sparkled and whose countenance became
livelier whenever the subject of music was broached. It is indis-
putable that the two men were friends and closely associated with
one another, although some of Lachner's anecdotes have not survived tests of historical accuracy; whether he embellished them in
old age, when his colourful tales first appeared, or whether memory simply played tricks on him, we cannot know.[3] He claimed the
closest of friendships in the great composer's last years, saying,
"The two of us, Schubert and I, shared our works with one

---

2. Hermann Mendel, *Musikalisches Conversations-Lexikon. Eine Encyklopädie der
gesammten musikalischen Wissenschaften*, vol. 6 (Berlin, 1876), p. 322.
3. For example, one "Herr S." relayed a tale entitled *Lebensgeschichtliche Anekdoten*
purportedly from Lachner in a special Schubert issue of the Stuttgart *Neue Musik-
Zeitung*, vol. 10, no. 12 (1889), p. 149, about an opera singer named Franz Siebert
(1793–1858) who stuck like a burr to the Nature-lovers Lachner and Schubert when
they were on a woodland walk in the hills surrounding Vienna. The two composers
then played a prank on the impossibly vain performer by inviting him to sing in a
glade where the echoes would enhance his gorgeous voice; while the male peacock
warbled away, Lachner and Schubert beat a swift retreat. But Siebert was at the
Kärntnertor Theater from mid-1818 to the end of 1821 and then did not return until
1829; since Lachner only arrived at the end of 1822 and Schubert died in 1828, the
chronology seems impossible.

another in sketches ... the hours, days, and months flew by in the happiest of dealings and in strivings devoid of jealousy, in the reciprocal exchange of thoughts and daily bulletins about what the Muse had bestowed on both of us".[4] Earlier, in a letter of 17 June 1854, he told his correspondent, "We [he and Schubert] were the best of friends, played our compositions for one another in the late morning and exchanged our views on the compositions with the greatest openness, whereby we both learned. In the afternoons, we would make excursions to nearby Grinzing, Klosterneuburg, etc. and often would not part until midnight, only to see each other the next morning. Since that time, I feel an emptiness in my musical strivings, a void that can no longer be filled."[5]

Whatever the occasionally shaky historical foundation for Lachner's reminiscences, these passages are rich in psychological revelation. One notes the assertion of equality with Schubert in their shared past, and indeed, the two men often appear together in Viennese publishers' announcements of new dance music for piano and of songs, in particular, dances for piano. Lachner is even singled out in the Mainz musical periodical *Cäcilia* for 1827 as a composer of "excellent sonatas", while Schubert is praised in the same sentence for his "beautiful songs", deemed a less weighty branch of composition in contemporary eyes.[6] But if Lachner, in later life, was proud of his association with bygone greatness, if he genuinely mourned the death of someone he dubbed "the most

---

4. Franz Lachner, *Erinnerungen an Schubert und Beethoven* in *Die Presse* (Vienna, 1 November 1881); a shortened version appears in Otto Erich Deutsch, *Die Erinnerungen seiner Freunde* (Leipzig, 1957), pp. 331–339. This small but potent portion of Lachner's memoirs is also cited in Günter Wagner, *Franz Lachner als Liederkomponist nebst einem biographischen Teil und dem thematischen Verzeichnis sämtlicher Lieder* (Giebing, 1970), p. 12.
5. Lachner's letter to Franz Dingelstedt's father, written in Munich on 17 June 1854, is reproduced in part in Deutsch, *Die Erinnerungen seiner Freunde*, pp. 225–226.
6. In Till Gerrit Waidelich, Renate Hilmar-Voit, and Andreas Mayer (eds.), *Franz Schubert: Dokumente 1817–1830*, vol. 1: *Texte* (Tutzing, 1993), items nos. 298 (p. 224), 311 (pp. 231–232), 364 (p. 261), 370 (p. 267), 430 (p. 298) and 439 (p. 302) are announcements of collections of dance music in which both Schubert and Lachner are to be found; in fact, in the *Sammlung 40 neuer Walzer* published by Weigl in 1824, Lachner composed the *Schlußwalzer mit Coda*. The notice in *Cäcilia* is cited in ibid., no. 436 (p. 301) and again, translated into English for London's *The Quarterly Musical Magazine and Review*, vol. 10, no. 38 (1829), pp. 183–189, in ibid., no. 677 (p. 468).

modest and unassuming of artists... the closest and dearest friend with whom I spent many hours",[7] one senses a certain subterranean jealousy in the latter-day invocation of "*neidlosem* Streben" and the statement that "we *both* learned" [italics mine]. Given the critics' comparisons of Lachner's songs to Schubert's and his symphonies to Beethoven's, any sympathetic person can understand the longer-lived, lesser composer's ambivalence. "[He] follows Schubert's path", one reviewer wrote in 1833, adding that Schubert was "original".[8] While the critic then goes on to praise Lachner for composing better songs than Schubert's, the palm for inventing a powerful new aesthetic of *Lied* composition goes to the dead, not the living, composer.

In his own day, Lachner enjoyed considerable critical approbation. Hermann Mendel in his *Musikalisches Conversations-Lexikon* hails him as "one of the foremost masters of music in the present day";[9] if this leaves an escape hatch for posterity to revise that judgment downward, it is high praise nevertheless. Once Lachner had flung his hat into the Wagnerian Ring as an opponent of *Gesamtkunstwerk*, it is difficult to find critiques not tainted by Wagnerism on one or the other side of the fence, but most of his songs were both composed and reviewed before the *Wagner-Streit* began. Like Schubert's, Lachner's fame in the first half of the century was based principally on his songs, although his larger instrumental works were noticed in reviews as well—in fact, before such recognition was accorded to his great contemporary's magnificent instrumental works from the final years. Gustav Schilling, in the fourth volume of his *Encylopädie der gesammten musikalischen Wissenschaften, oder Universal-Lexicon der Tonkunst*, wrote in 1837 that Lachner's *Das Waldvöglein*, Op. 28, no. 1 on a poem by Johann Nikolaus Vogel was sung everywhere in Austria and would perhaps guarantee Lachner's fame there forever.[10] Other ency-

---

7. This is what Lachner told Heinrich Kreissle von Hellborn for the latter man's *Franz Schubert* (Vienna, 1865), p. 452.
8. From a review of Lachner's *Sängerfahrt*, op. 33, Parts 1 and 2, in *Caecilia: Eine Zeitschrift für die musikalische Welt*, vol. 15 (1833), p. 190.
9. Hermann Mendel, *Musikalisches Conversations-Lexikon. Eine Encyklopädie der gesammten musikalischen Wissenschaften* (Berlin, 1876), vol. 6, p. 212.

clopaedists agreed, with Ferdinand Simon Gaßner stating in the *Universal-Lexikon der Tonkunst* of 1849 that Lachner's *Lieder* were his most distinctive and brilliant works, especially the concert songs with obbligato accompaniment by horn or cello or violin.[11] The fashion for such songs drew fire from some: a dyspeptic critic for the *Allgemeine musikalische Zeitung* in 1833 scolded Lachner for grinding out still more specimens of a genre he found objectionable: "Diese fast in alle Akademien sich einschmüggelnden Gesänge mit Klaviergeklimper und Horn- oder Violoncell- oder Fagottbrühe fangen nachgerade an im Konzertsaal gar gewaltig eklig zu werden".[12] But, says Günter Wagner, Lachner's most recent biographer (and how ironic that Lachner would have a biographer with this name), peevishness of this order was rare. Most, like Mendel, praise Lachner's songs for their "great warmth of expression, their singability and truthfulness to Nature, as well as the idiosyncratic and powerful shaping of the harmonies", and they wax particularly lyrical over Lachner's mastery of counterpoint. He does not, they write, consider contrapuntal devices an end unto themselves but rather uses them to beautiful aesthetic ends.[13] Over thirty years earlier, in the *Allgemeine musikalische Zeitung* for 1844, another critic was already praising Lachner's learning:

[This composer's songs are appreciated] in part for their almost always felicitous, fresh and expressive quality, in part for a certain assured solidity of musical handling and development of the chosen motives, by which this composer makes of even the smallest song, be it earnest or merry in its contents, a fully rounded, complete work of art, in which the practiced eye can with pleasure detect many refined traces of a master's pen.

---

10. Gustav Schilling, *Enzyklopädie der gesammten musikalischen Wissenschaften, oder Universal-Lexicon der Tonkunst*, vol. 4 (Stuttgart, 1837), p. 294. The Aríon Trio has recently recorded eight of Lachner's songs with obbligato horn, including *Waldvöglein*. See *Schubert & Co. – Romantische Lieder für Sopran, Horn und Klavier*, Antes Edition CD 31.9120 (1998).

11. Ferdinand Simon Gaßner, *Universal Lexikon der Tonkunst* (Stuttgart, 1849), p. 521.

12. *Allgemeine musikalische Zeitung*, vol. 35 (Leipzig, 1833), Spaltung 395.

13. Mendel, *Musikalisches Conversations-Lexikon*, p. 214.

The incorporation of contrapuntal devices into *Lieder*—Schubert does it, Lachner does it, Schumann does it, and so do many others—is one aspect of nineteenth-century song that awaits further scholarly investigation.

Anyone perusing the Lachner song catalogue is immediately struck by the preponderance of Heine settings during the early years.[14] If Schubert, as I have speculated elsewhere, cast Heine off in revulsion after the brief, brilliant fling that produced six masterpieces,[15] Lachner's infatuation lasted longer. All of his extant Heine songs were composed after Schubert's death (he may, of course, have destroyed earlier settings), and one can make of the chronological lapse between that tragic event and Lachner's 1831–1832 spate of song composition what one will. He set only two of the six poems Schubert had selected, *Du schönes Fischermädchen* and *Ich stand in dunklen Träumen*, and neither of his creations can hold a candle to Schubert's darker imaginings; but away from the greater composer's turf, he could and did accomplish more. In 1831 alone, he composed thirty Heine songs, including the concert-song *Neuer Frühling* with obbligato cello or horn, op. 27, no. 1; the important song cycle *Sängerfahrt*, op. 33, with sixteen Heine songs; a setting of *Lore-Ley* (*Ich weiß nicht, was soll es bedeuten*) in his *Zwölf deutsche Gesänge*, op. 35; and five Heine songs in the *Sechs deutsche Gesänge*, op. 49.[16] Such a quantity of Heine songs in a single year is a testament both to this poet's utility for "progressive" song composers and to Schubert's influence on those with ears to hear and minds to comprehend.

---

14. In R. Hirsch's beautifully-produced *Album für Gesang mit Original Beiträgen von A. H. Chelard, J. W. Kalliwoda, F. Lachner, C. Loewe, Mendelssohn-Bartholdy, G. Meyerbeer, F. Schneider, C. Kreutzer, P. Lindpaintner, H. Marschner, A. Methfessel, C. G. Reissiger, R. Schumann, L. Spohr* (Leipzig, 1842), one finds Lachner's *Der Sclave* (pp. 22–24), poem by L. Koch.

15. Schubert's engagement with Heine is discussed in the first chapter of the author's *Heinrich Heine and the Lied*, pp. 1–88 (see note no. 1).

16. See Günter Wagner's *Thematisches Verzeichnis Sämtlicher Lieder Franz Lachners* in the same author's *Franz Lachner als Liederkomponist*, pp. 143–304. There is also the *Drei Lieder nach Gedichten von H. Heine für eine Singstimme, Violoncello und Klavierbegleitung*, op. 34; the two songs *Mitternacht* and *Die Rätsel* from the *Drei deutsche Gesänge für eine Singstimme, Violoncello und Klavierbegleitung*, op. 36; and the songs *Ihre Gestalt* and *Fragen* from the *Sechs deutsche Gesänge für eine Bariton- oder Altstimme mit Klavierbegleitung*, op. 54.

It is the first of Lachner's two cycles entitled *Sängerfahrt* that most interests me at the moment because it includes one magnificent song and several other fine specimens. In the review of op. 33 already cited from *Caecilia* for 1833, the reviewer wrote that Lachner, like Schubert, demonstrates "a pronounced tendency for the pictorial depiction of those emotional situations in which a certain tender intimacy of the mind [is] awakened and evoked by the outward natural milieu or in strife with external circumstances".[17] But Lachner is superior, this writer declares, because his accompaniments are "nicht so schroff" and because he does not repeat accompanimental figuration to the point of exhaustion.[18] The reviewer goes on to complain that the poet's name is nowhere to be found, and indeed, Heine is not identified either on the title page or at the ends of individual songs, as was customary.[19] One wonders whether Tobias Haslinger, the publisher of both Schubert's *Schwanengesang* four years earlier and Lachner's op. 33, might have feared difficulties with the censors. If Heine was already controversial in the 1820s, he was more so by 1833 when these songs were published, two years prior to the poet's Damnatur from the Prussian censors. Heine would complain in his later years that too many composers availed themselves of his verse without acknowledging the source of the words, and one wonders if he knew of Lachner's first *Sängerfahrt*.

When the third and final Heft of this cycle appeared in print (the review cited above treats the first two sections), the critic once again invoked the relationship to the "so vielfältig hochgefeierten Franz Schubert" and again proclaimed Lachner's superiority.[20] While we would not agree with this particular critic nowadays, the ninth song in *Sängerfahrt*— *Wasserfahrt*—deserves every bit of the renewed attention it is now receiving from artists such as

---

17. *Caecilia*, vol. 15, op. cit., pp. 190–191.
18. Ibid., p. 191.
19. Ibid., p. 190.
20. In ibid., p. 194, the reviewer for *Caecilia* describes *Wasserfahrt* as the tale of a lover departing the Fatherland and hoping in vain for a glimpse of his beloved—in other words, he takes it literally. "Completely in Schubert's style", he writes, saying that the piano figuration depicts both outer and inner worlds with great power. "Die Stimme ist schwierig vorzutragen", he adds.

Christoph Prégardien and Andreas Staier, although there is not yet a modern edition of the score, long out-of-print.[21] The text is the fourteenth poem from the *Junge Leiden* section in Heine's first volume of *Gedichte* (1822) and in the *Buch der Lieder* (1827), a poem that foreshadows motifs also found in *Ich stand in dunklen Träumen.*

Wasserfahrt	Journey by Water
I Ich stand gelehnet an den Mast,	I stood leaning against the mast,
Und zählte jede Welle.	And counted every wave.
Ade! mein schönes Vaterland!	Farewell, my beautiful Fatherland!
Mein Schiff, das segelt schnelle!	My ship, it sails swiftly!
Ich kam schön Liebchens	I passed by the beautiful
Haus vorbei,	beloved's house,
Die Fensterscheiben blinken;	The windowpanes gleam;
Ich guck' mir fast die Augen aus,	I practically stare my eyes out,
Doch will mir niemand winken.	But no one will beckon to me.
Ihr Tränen, bleibt mir aus dem Aug',	You tears, stay out of my eyes
Daß ich nicht dunkel sehe,	That I not see darkly.
Mein krankes Herz, brich mir nicht	My sick heart, don't break
Vor allzugroßem Wehe.[22]	From all-too-great sorrow.

One of Heine's friends in his early days, Johann Baptist Rousseau, recounted an anecdote in 1840 about his famous acquaintance, a tale in which some have seen the origins both of *Warte, warte, wilder Schiffsmann* and *Wasserfahrt*. Rousseau's Catholic-mystic Romanticism was something Heine quickly outgrew, thereafter mocking such Christian apologists in verse, but in their salad days, the two men were literary confrères. In his *Living Pictures*, published in the *Omnibus zwischen Rhein und Niemen*, Rousseau wrote that Heine, during his mercantile apprenticeship in

---

21. I was led to this song by the marvelous rendition from Christoph Prégardien, tenor, and Andreas Staier, fortepiano, performing *Beethoven–Kruffi–Lachner Lieder* on Teldec/Das Alte Werk 3984–21473–2 (1999).
22. Heinrich Heine, *Gedichte* (Berlin, 1822), pp. 99–100, and the same author, *Buch der Lieder* (Hamburg, 1827) p. 78.

Hamburg, conceived the notion of sailing away with a band of other like-minded young men to find and colonize an island, like Prospero Frescobaldi—a "natural man" in whom courage, energy, and sexual potency unite—in Johann Wilhelm Heinse's *Ardinghello und die glückseligen Inseln* of 1787. The police got wind of the scheme, and Heine's uncle Salomon must, so Rousseau reports, have had to lay out a pretty penny to recoup the outlay for provisions. But Salomon was supposedly so amused at his nephew's romantic adventurism that he agreed to finance the young man's education at the University of Bonn. "From two maidens I take my leave", Heine proclaims in *Warte, warte, wilder Schiffsmann*, "from Europe and from you", and one notes the order of priority. Rousseau writes that Heine was twenty years old at the time, and in 1817, his cousin Amalie, or "Molly", was much on his mind, as was poetry. But there is no autograph manuscript for Heine's *Wasserfahrt*, and the speculation that it was written "some time between 1818 and 1821" leaves room for a genesis whose *raison d'être* is, I suspect, deeper and darker than the putative island-Utopia of Rousseau's reminiscence.[23] There are reasons beyond frustrated love to leave home.

The stance at the start of *Wasserfahrt* may be Odyssean, but nothing else bespeaks the antique hero.[24] Where, in the episode of the Sirens, the hyper-masculine, ultra-rational Odysseus (Enlightenment Man *avant la lettre*) has himself bound by an act of will to the ship's mast—one of the more obvious phallic symbols in all of literature—Heine's devastated persona keeps breakdown at bay by means of obsessive rituals and by arranging words into poetic shapes. From the ship that bears him away, he counts the waves, masochistically measuring the distance from his homeland. In this poem, Heine imagines exile long before he fled the German-speaking world for Paris. What might those first moments of the voyage be like, in transition between the known

---

23. See Heinrich Heine, *Säkularausgabe*, vol. 1: *Gedichte 1812–1827, Kommentar*, part 1, ed. by Hans Böhm (Berlin, 1982), pp. 195–196.
24. In poem no. 11 of *Die Heimkehr, Der Sturm spielt auf zum Tanze*, the persona also clings to the mast: "Ich halte mich fest am Mastbaum, / Und wünsche: wär' ich zu Haus" (stanza 3, lines 3 and 4).

and the unknown? The counting demarcates distance not only in space but in the time between Then and Now; when the poet counts, he imitates the ticking clock that bears everyone away from what they love and eventually from life itself. Departing the homeland where an ideal died, the persona dives headlong into the first stages of grief, recounted with a clinician's accuracy. Frantic energy futilely expended, obsession with what was lost, the fear that one will actually die from the physical stress of mourning: it is all here. So too is the separation of self into one who suffers and one who observes and records, evident in the tiny detail of the word "das" in line 4 ("Mein Schiff, das segelt schnelle"). "My ship" (the familiar Homeric symbol of the individual life on a voyage through the ocean of Time) becomes 'it' in a masterful revision of the line as it appears in the 1822 *Gedichte*, "Mein Schiffchen segelt schnelle". One is also grateful for the 1827 deletion of the fourth and fifth stanzas, which Heine struck out in the copy of the 1822 text that he used to make corrections for later publication:[25] "Stolziere nicht du falsche Maid, / Ich will's meiner Mutter sagen; / Wenn meine Mutter mich weinen sieht, / Dann brauch' ich nicht lange zu klagen. / / Meine Mutter singt mir ein Wiegenlied vor, / Bis ich schlafe und erbleiche; / Doch dich schleppt sie Nachts bey den Haaren herbey, / Und zeigt dir meine Leiche". How very adolescent these reproaches are!—"My mother will make you pay... you'll be sorry when I'm dead". The excision of these stanzas allows the themes of homeland and exile to step to the fore in a grown-up incarnation, its traumas now of the adult variety.

This poet veils the cause of the persona's exile in literary fictions, although he drops enough hints for those aware of his "Maskenfreiheit" to decode the actual source of his grief. The censors he so wittily dubbed as fools ("Die deutschen Censoren ———————————————Dummköpfe———", he wrote[26])

---

25. This Arbeitsexemplar of the 1822 *Gedichte* is in the collection of the Heinrich-Heine-Institut in Düsseldorf, with corrections by Friedrich Merckel as well as Heine, and served as preparation for the 1827 *Buch der Lieder*.
26. The famous passage about the German censors constitutes the entirety of chapter 12 of *Ideen. Das Buch LeGrand* of 1826. See Heinrich Heine, *Säkularausgabe*, vol. 5: *Reisebilder I 1824–1828*, ed. by Karl Wolfgang Becker (Berlin, 1970), p. 116.

would not have been amused had his persona made explicit the political implications at the heart of the poem. *Wasserfahrt* operates, I would speculate, on at least two levels, one overt and one covert, in Heine's typical fashion. On the face of it, this poet spins yet another variation on the antique theme of the despairing lover whose sweetheart has rejected him and who flees the land where his love came to naught; but beneath this topmost layer are charged personal and political meanings bound together. The figures on the surface are manipulated at the behest of the subterranean agenda that could not be named openly. The "schön Liebchen", for example, is a nameless, faceless archetype who seems to have strayed into this poem from German folk poetry, and her lack of any human particularity in *Wasserfahrt* points the way to a more symbolic identity. It matters that it is not to *her* but to her *house* that the persona comes, there to stare through the windows until his eyes practically pop out of his head, to use the colloquialism perhaps closest to Heine's "Ich guck" mir fast die Augen aus'. The verb "gucken" is not what early nineteenth-century readers would expect in elevated poetic art. Here, Heine might have taken his cue from Wilhelm Müller's *Die schöne Müllerin*, whose frantic miller lad peers through the window pane in *Erster Schmerz, letzter Scherz* (one of the three poems from the narrative that Schubert did not set to music) and sees the miller maid and hunter in flagrante delicto.[27] There is a crucial difference, however, between the two scenarios: Müller's Peeping Tom, driven to voyeurism by despair, has lost his "Liebchen", but Heine's persona has not. This supremely clever poet allows readers to assume loss of the beloved as well as country, and yet nowhere

---

27. The relevant stanzas of *Erster Schmerz, letzter Scherz* are the fourth and fifth (of ten): "Die Fensterscheiben glänzen / Im klaren Morgenschein, / Und hinter den Fensterscheiben / Da sitzt die Liebste main. / / Ein Jäger, ein grüner Jäger, / Der liegt in ihrem Arm—/ Ei, Bach, wie lustig du rauschest! / Ei, Sonne, wie scheinst du so warm!" Heine must have pounced on this work hot off the press, as Wilhelm Müller's *Sieben- und siebzig Gedichte aus den hinterlassenen Papieren eines reisenden Waldhornisten* (the title is a send-up of Romantic themes) came out the previous year (Dessau, 1821). See the author's *Schubert, Müller and Die schöne Müllerin* (Cambridge, 1997), pp. 174–178.

does Heine say so outright. But both poets' personae desire what they cannot have, while those inside the house acknowledge neither man.

And they never will. Heine's choice of verb tenses is always precise, especially when he treats Time; the persona went (imperfect past) to the beloved's house, where no one will (pointing into the future) beckon him to come in. Behind the barrier separating those inside the house from those outside is an implicit refusal to grant the desperate speaker admittance, despite his entreating gaze. The order in which images and themes are presented is also precisely plotted, and here, the farewell to the Fatherland precedes the reference to the sweetheart and the inhabitants of the house. It is possible to interpret the beloved as German poetry (truly Heine's beloved), her house as Germany itself, and those within it as German citizens who will not admit the Jew Heine, despite his midnight conversion to Protestantism on 28 June 1825, when he became Christian (an ironic choice of name) Johann Heinrich Heine—a decision he instantly regretted.[28] "I assure you", he wrote his friend Moses Moser on 19 December 1825, "that had the laws allowed the theft of silver spoons, I would not have had myself baptized".[29] Heine himself knew that he was temperamentally unsuited for those occupations in which he tried to find an entrée (the law, university teaching) and did not want to practise law, not really.[30] But the fact remains that conversion was a necessity for admission into those professions in which one could earn a living as an educated man - and even then, Jewishness was not so easily expunged. No Christian baptismal font could wash away awareness of "the 5,588 Years' War", the year 1827 being 5,588

---

28. In S. S. Prawer, *Heine's Jewish Comedy: A Study of his Portraits of Jews and Judaism* (Oxford, 1985), pp. 106–107, Prawer points out that in the *Harzreise*, a business-rival of the poet's uncle Salomon Heine, a man named Lazarus Gumpel, is caricatured as Christian Gumpel.

29. See Heinrich Heine, *Säkularausgabe*, vol. 20: *Briefe 1815–1831*, ed. by Fritz Eisner (Berlin, 1970), p. 227.

30. In a letter of 6 December 1825, Heine sends Rudolf Christiani a copy of his poem *Sie liebten sich beide* and then says, "Aber wirklich, Christiany, nachdem Du dieses Lied gelesen hast glaubst Du noch wirklich daß ich hier Advokat werde?" See ibid., p. 225.

according to the Jewish calendar established by Hillel II in the fourth century. In *Ideen: Das Buch LeGrand*, Heine ironically proclaimed his adherence to the "party of reasonable and rational men", who had been "for 5,588 years... at war with the party of fools".[31] This is yet another of Heine's multifarious cloaked ways of referring to his origins, and so too, I believe, is the scenario in *Wasserfahrt*. He would always have been the outsider looking in, and he knew it well before his flight to France.

Heine uses the same adjective "schön" for both the Fatherland and the sweetheart, linking the two in shared beauty, but what exactly was this Fatherland he names both as beautiful and as his? There was no such thing as a unified Germany until 1871, and yet, the word "Vaterland" appears in print long before the nation-state became a reality. What it designates is the desire for a collective common ground unified by king, God, land, and language, but the specific shape of the thing desired could, and did, take many forms in the imaginations of those who wished for it.[32] By the last half of the eighteenth century, one could read in poems, philosophical treatises, newspapers, and almanacs of an Enlightened Fatherland built on reason and freedom, but one could also find bristling, blood-soaked visions of an entity with the right to demand an individual's life in sacrifice to the State. In a treatise first published in 1761 and entitled *Vom Tode für das Vaterland*, for example, the Prussian philosopher Thomas Abbt harnesses the concept of a fatherland to an absolutist monarchy and calls on analogies to ancient Rome for his assertions of masculine duty to military defence of the nation.[33] As a cultural entity, the

---

31. Prawer, *Heine's Jewish Comedy*, entitles his second chapter (pp. 97–127) *The 5,588 Years' War*. The citation comes from chapter 15 of *Ideen. Das Buch LeGrand*; see Heine, *Säkularausgabe*, vol. 5, p. 127.
32. See Abigail Green, *Fatherlands: State-Building and Nationhood in Nineteenth-Century Germany* (Cambridge, 2001), "Introduction," pp. 1–21; John Breuilly (ed.), *The state of Germany. The national idea in the making, unmaking and remaking of a modern nation state* (London, 1992); Peter Krüger, ed., *Deutschland, deutscher Staat, deutsche Nation. Historische Erkundungen eines Spannungsverhältnisses* (Marburg, 1993); and Hagen Schulze, *The course of German nationalism, from Frederick to Bismarck 1763–1867* (Cambridge, 1991).
33. Thomas Abbt, *Vom Tode für das Vaterland* (Berlin, 1761).

Fatherland had existed for centuries, but as a political and ideological entity, the word assumed new meanings (often quite vague) in the wake of the Napoleonic wars, especially when the new German Confederation failed to fulfil the nationalist aspirations aroused by the resistance to Napoleon. Heine despised the ancien régime and was hardly a proponent for its return, but he also saw the dark side of the new Teutonic nationalism sooner than almost anyone else. With breathtaking economy, he makes *his* choice of vision apparent by means of the adjective "beautiful".

But Heine recognized that *his* Fatherland was incompatible with the new ideologies of nationhood; those rulers who wished to suppress all subversive elements did not share his view of what Germany should be. Like a spurned lover, he simultaneously lashed out in retaliatory fury against the Germany that would not have him and longed for *his* Germany — its folklore, its poetry, even its food — in unbounded wistfulness. It was a torment that began early. In one of his most famous letters, addressed to his friend Christian Sethe on 14 April 1822, he writes:

Alles was deutsch ist, ist mir zuwider … Alles Deutsche wirkt auf mich wie ein Brechpulver. Die deutsche Sprache zerreißt meine Ohre. Die eignen Gedichte ekeln mich zuweilen an, wenn ich sehe, daß sie auf deutsch geschrieben sind. Sogar das Schreiben dieses Billets wird mir sauer, weil die deutschen Schriftzüge schmerzhaft auf meine Nerven wirken. Je n'aurais jamais cru que les bêtes qu'on nomme allemands soient une race si ennuyante et malicieuse en même temps.[34]

The epistolary fantasy-cum-temper tantrum romps on in French, as he imagines leaving Germany and going to Märchen-Romantic Arabia, where he will create Persian poems while leading "une vie pastorale". But at the time of this letter, he was still in Germany, nine years away from self-imposed exile in France. There, for all his delight in things Parisian, the realities of exile hit home. His poem, *Ich hatte einst ein schönes Vaterland*, is one of the most potent evocations of an exile's nostalgia, of a writer's rue, ever written.

---

34. Heinrich Heine, *Säkularausgabe*, vol. 20, p. 50.

Ich hatte einst ein schönes Vaterland.	I once had a beautiful fatherland.
Der Eichenbaum	The oak trees
Wuchs dort so hoch,	grew so high there,
die Veilchen nickten sanft.	the little violets nodded gently.
Es war ein Traum.	It was a dream.
Das küßte mich auf deutsch	It kissed me in German and spoke
und sprach auf deutsch	in German
(Man glaubt es kaum	(one hardly believes
Wie gut es klang) das Wort:	how good it sounded) the Word:
"Ich liebe dich!"	"I love you!"
Es war ein Traum.[35]	It was a dream.

This dream — not Romantic fairy tale fantasy, but simply something wished for, a more heartbreaking use of the word — is foreshadowed by poems such as *Wasserfahrt*, in which exile is a fresh, raw prospect, producing panic. The tone of sad resignation in the later masterpiece is not yet possible.

Could Lachner have been aware of the political gelignite discernible in his chosen poem if one reads it from a certain angle? Or does he take it at face value as the latest version of the ages-old theme of the rejected lover? However he imputed the cause of the despair in this poem, he was clearly captivated by the challenge of rendering into music an extreme psychological state. How does one make sonorous the repetitive-ritualistic behaviour that keeps grief from killing the persona outright, if only just barely? Lachner seized on the compositional possibilities that the three words

---

35. Heinrich Heine, vol. 2: *Gedichte 1827–1844 und Versepen*, ed. by Irmgard Möller and Hans Böhm (Berlin, 1979), p. 66. There are very few musical settings of this elegiac masterpiece; perhaps the focus on language itself is such that music cannot find sufficient elbow room. Every detail compels: one notes the arboreal symbol of Germany grown tall, its elevation symbolic of greatness, with what one imagines of multiples of Goethe's violets sheltered beneath it. The enjambed "aside", ("Man glaubt es kaum / Wie gut es klang"), interrupts a complete sentence ("Das küßte mich auf deutsch und sprach auf deutsch das Wort: 'Ich liebe Dich!'"), and the placement of the break-in is poignant. The phrase follows immediately upon the doubled word "deutsch" as a way of insisting that only German can elicit such a profound response from this persona. The designation of the words (plural), "Ich liebe dich!" as "das Wort" tells us that when Germany speaks of love for its poets, those words are Holy Writ.

"zählte jede Welle" gave him for the fusion of the stylized-pictor-ial, the psychological-dramatic, and the musically radical; if he learned how to do so from Schubert, he learned it well. What he manages to capture in the piano figuration we hear throughout *Wasserfahrt* is both the jittery restlessness of fresh grief and the attempt to exert control over a life spun out-of-control by mark-ing time and measuring distance. Lachner's astute decisions for his rendition of this poem begin when he dispenses with a piano introduction as a discrete entity of the sort customary in most nineteenth-century songs. Instead, with a single wave, a single bar, we are plunged in medias res into frantic counting. In the one-bar figure which we hear over and over again in the piano, rhythmic tensions and dissonance hyper-activate a harmonic progression monomanaically limited at the start of it all (Ex. 1). The utmost stylization of a small wave rising-and-falling that we see and hear in the right-hand part is something perceived through the scrim of

Example 1. Franz Lachner. "Wasserfahrt", mm. 1-9, from Sängerfahrt, Op. 33. Vienna, Tobias Haslinger.

a disturbed mind, Lachner thus subsuming onomatopoeia into an emotional state made sonorous. In fact, this is something akin to a mad dance, the reiterated, syncopated bass rhythmic pattern being fancifully describable as a *danse hongroise* on speed; Lachner might have known it from the climactic final section of Schubert's *Divertissement à l'hongroise*. That the right hand scrambles into action just after the downbeat in the left hand adds to the near-psychotic aura of it all, and Lachner charges each bar with still more high-voltage rhythmic tension when he stresses beat 2 by means both of the grace-noted accentuation of the right-hand appoggiatura figures and the prolongational emphasis in the bass. Beat 3 is made electric by the leap upwards in the right hand and by the mid-bar accent at the apex of the leap. The dissonance created on that second, ordinarily weak, beat by the grace-noted appoggiatura in the right hand in conjunction with the tonic chord, such that the pitches B C D and E briefly sound together in stinging acerbity, is another telling detail of the figure. So, too, is the right hand's avoidance of the tonic pitch until the fourth and weakest beat of the bar. That a tonic chord—-that is all we hear in bb. 1–3—can be made to sound so charged is a considerable feat.

But perhaps the most ingenious compositional choice Lachner made, one he maintains throughout the song, is the discrepancy between the metre as written and as performed. A vocal melody notated in crotchets, minims, and semibreves has to sound as if those durations were actually cut in half and then sung at a frenetic pace. In other words, the song is in hyper-metre, such that a single four-beat unit or hyper-bar in performance is here notated as two bars; looking at Ex. 1, one sees that b. 2 in the vocal line is an anacrusis figure to the single "bar" in bb. 3 and 4. Lachner does so, I would conjecture, for profoundly poetic reasons. The way this music looks on the printed page is essential to its meanings; if the repeated figures in the piano each consumed only half-a-bar, we would not be forced by the barlines on either side to count each motive/bar as a single unit, as one musical wavelet. What Lachner's notation does is to reinforce visually the performers' awareness of the persona's counting compulsion. A listener with no access to the score can certainly hear motivic repetition, but those who *see* these pages are brought even closer to the fraught state of mind which Lachner converts into music. In this brilliant notational conceit, music which looks slower when measured by these conventional-looking note values, as if by clock and calendar, actually speeds by at a frantic pace, carrying one farther and farther away from lost love. It matters that the piano part never rests for an instant until the end, that every beat is filled with sound, as if with adrenaline and racing blood.

The way in which this song is chained at its beginning to a repeated tonic chord might remind some people of Schubert's *Gretchen am Spinnrade*, another song of subjectivity in turmoil. In that famous work, Schubert harps on the tonic harmony for ten bars and then jumps suddenly to the chord on the flatted seventh degree, followed by a diminished seventh clashing with the continued flatted seventh pitch in the bass; shocking for 1814, the passage has lost none of its capacity to startle. In Lachner's *Wasserfahrt*, the only divergence from the tonic chord in bb. 1–6 is formed by neighbouring motion on either side of tonic, in which the leading tone D-sharp in the bass grates briefly against the grace-note-accented D-natural in the right-hand figure; this is the first instance of the important D-natural / D-sharp dichotomy throughout the song. Mutability being the law both of life and of music, the tonality must eventually change, and here, it begins to do so at the words of farewell ("Leb' wohl"). Lachner realized that the persona's anguish is due to loss of the Fatherland he had wrongly thought was his, and therefore he makes the approach to that word the modulatory corridor to the dominant, while the word itself is the first climactic point in a song which races pell-mell from one such instant to another. Lachner simply jumps, quite Schubert-like, to B *minor* at the words "Leb' wohl", where the dynamics are made revelatory of stream-of-consciousness processes in the mind. In the middle of the singer's softly chanted "Farewell", the piano is, for the first time, loud—suddenly so. The impression is that first word of parting immediately impels a rush of strong feeling even before the two small words "Leb' wohl" have flown by. The fact that the vocal line is always inside the piano part, with the right-hand figures washing over the singer's melody at all times, heightens the effect of this sudden *forte* eruption in the accompaniment (Ex. 2). Did Lachner learn the musical transcription of subjectivity from Schubert? One thinks of the miller lad in *Die böse Farbe* from *Die schöne Müllerin* leaping up to the third syllable of "toten*bleich*" in shocked realization that he is envisaging his own death and realizes that Lachner had precursors in his own city, his own circle of friends, for what happens in bb. 10–11 of *Wasserfahrt*.

By now, one expects that the word at the heart of the song, "Vaterland", should impel another stage of emotional ramping-up, a strong reaction of some sort, and it does. As the singer repeats, "Leb' wohl", en route to naming the object of his goodbyes, a crescendo swells to *fortissimo* at the word itself, and minor mode

Example 2. Franz Lachner. "Wasserfahrt", mm. 10–24, from Sängerfahrt, Op. 33. Vienna, Tobias Haslinger.

changes to the brightness of B major. Lachner, like Schubert, could make the familiar Mozartian dichotomy of parallel minor and major modes mean something other than the more hackneyed uses of the convention in song, such as happy past/major mode and unhappy present/minor mode. The Fatherland as something warm, beautiful, gleaming in major mode becomes here a kind of hysteri-

cal brightness. The adjective "schönes" sounds to a B minor harmony, while the noun it modifies is in the major; the shadowed reference to beauty qualifies the brightness that follows. Each detail of
change in bb. 14–24 (the end of stanza 1 and the first section of the
song) is finely-calibrated to tell of near-hysteria: the singer runs the
appellation of "mein schönes Vaterland" directly into "mein Schiff"
with no break, or at most, room for only a snatched intake of air
between what, in the poem, are two separate phrases on two different lines. In doing so, Lachner sets "Va – [terland]" and "Schiff" to
the same high F-sharp in an implicit claim that they should be the
same, that the persona's ship/self should be anchored in the
Fatherland but is not, is sailing away instead. The danse hongroise
offbeat pattern in the bass gives way to a more symmetrical pattern
of four crotchets, paving the way for the setting of stanza 2, and the
vocal line rises to the passagio, the "break" in tenor and soprano
voices, and lives there for nine bars. The inherent taut, somewhat
shrill quality, the tension of the passagio tessitura, could not be more
right for these words and this place in the song.

Given the frenetic pace, the persona's panic, and the brevity of
the poem, Lachner repeats much of Heine's text. And yet, his persona only sings the first two lines of stanzas 1 and 3 once; the last
half of those verses is what impels horror-struck reiterations,
expressive both of incredulity and incitement to even greater grief.
Lachner divides the second stanza into two halves, the text of each
half repeated immediately in the wake of the initial statement. For
the first half, with its remembered pilgrimage to the beloved's
house, Lachner moves into a multivalent treble register, a femin-
ized and ethereal plane of illusion, and into parallel major mode,
that venerable song-symbol for bygone happiness. He also alters
the character of the figuration in the right hand, banishing the
mid-bar leaps and insistent accents, smoothing the figures out,
harmonizing them in mellifluous thirds and sixths, replacing *fortissimo* dynamics with the *pianissimo* of recollection, underpinning
the words "[Liebchens] Haus" with prayerful subdominant harmonies, such that we understand the house as something revered,
even now. And yet, the repeated chordal pulsations in the left-
hand part continue telling of obsession; however soft, they convey
something of the same daemonic energy as the repeated octave

pulsations beneath the Erlking's blandishments in Schubert's Op. 1. The incessant motion, the claustrophobia, the refusal of rests: Lachner maintains it all as before. Furthermore, the voicing of the cadential harmonies in bb. 34–35, at the verb "blinken", is notable for the prevalence of hollow perfect intervals and tritones in both hands, combining to produce two bars filled with dissonance and reflections. In an instance of dark musical wit, Lachner takes the ostinato repeated pitches in the lower voice of the right-hand part and the moving voice that outlines a third and returns to its point of origin (b. 34) and reverses them in mirror image in b. 35 (Ex. 3). Both voices in both bars are poised atop intervallic emptiness, above drumbeats in the left hand that sound fatalistic even in the treble register and played at such speed. The ways in which Schubert voices his harmonies and creates from the inter-

Example 3. Franz Lachner. "Wasserfahrt", mm. 27–39, from Sängerfahrt, Op. 33. Vienna, Tobias Haslinger.

play of linear voices a complex register of poetic events are part and parcel of his influence on other composers, and certainly so where song was at issue.

Heine's finely-calibrated changes of verb tense in stanza 2 demonstrate how memory is brought into the present and reactivated, to shattering effect. "I *came* to the sweetheart's house... I almost *stare* my eyes out", the persona says. (Either Lachner or Haslinger changed the colloquial verb "gucken" to the more conventional "schauen", possibly for reasons of greater singability.) In the recesses of his mind, he continues to see the negation and refusal that lie beyond those windowpanes. The contours of the beloved's house are still audible in the repeated quarter-note intervals of a third thrumming away in the left hand, but the grace-noted figuration in the right hand from earlier in the song returns. The leaping interval is now expanded to an octave (beginning in b. 44), paving the way for the whirlwind compounded of octave figuration at the end of the song. Lachner's persona twice sings of staring as hard as he can at mysterious people within the house who do not acknowledge him, and the composer inflects each statement of those words differently. There is great psychological acuity at work in his decision to make the initial statement redolent of rising hysteria, as if the persona can hardly believe the dreadful thing he is saying, and the second statement quieter, as if taking it in, admitting its terrible verity. The first time (bb. 44–51), Lachner sounds a harmonic trill in the piano, an embellishment of the dominant harmony, but with no resolution; we are suspended in tonal mid-air throughout this passage. In this uneasily-activated dominant, the G-naturals that first appear at the word "Augen" begin the process of negating the E major tonality of the "Liebchens Haus", which we realize in retrospect is the Fatherland; what the persona sees — or, rather, does not see — with his own eyes makes E major impossible for him. The clash of the downbeat accented D-sharp in the vocal line at the first syllables of "*Au* – gen" and "*win* – ken" against E in the bass tells of eyes in agony, of pain at the lack of response (bb. 46 and 50), and the dissonance is as harsh as any in Schubert's songs. The brightness of a beneficent Fatherland cannot be this persona's tonal climate, except briefly and then only as an illusion remembered through a scrim of grief.

When Lachner repeats these same words in bb. 51–59, he changes emphasis in a manner revelatory both of his close reading of Heine's poem and, I would speculate, his empathy with the experience it records (Ex. 4). He knew, after all, what it was not to be accorded recognition in his native country and to feel impelled to seek his fortune elsewhere, although his youthful experience of

Example 4. Franz Lachner. "Wasserfahrt", mm. 23–59, from Sängerfahrt, Op. 33. Vienna, Tobias Haslinger.

such things could not ultimately hold a candle to Heine's insoluble dilemma of Jewish identity in an anti-Jewish Germany. The harmonic trill in the left hand continues, but reharmonized; the deceptive manoeuvre, the semitone jolt upwards to a C major harmony (VI in E minor), and the sudden hush all lead us back to the original key. This time, it is not "eyes" and "beckon" that are stressed in the singer's melody but the word "fast", and the emphasis is an eloquent index of intensity, of the persona's fervent desire to be seen, acknowledged, and brought inside those rooms where his native country houses its honoured poets. Earlier, at the first statement of the words, "doch will mir niemand winken", we heard a crescendo of Angst, but now there is recognition of futility in the approach to half-cadence in E minor—we are no longer in tonal limbo (bb. 58–59)—and the diminuendo. Saying dreadful truth softly, to oneself, is more final-sounding than wracked loudness, and it brings the persona back to his own tonal realm. But despair rises to new heights immediately thereafter (the piano interlude in bb. 59–65) in this fever-chart of a song. The stern fact that "no one will beckon to me" is the trigger, the flashpoint, for an immense outburst of angry grief in reaction.

On the brink of succumbing to overwhelming emotion, the persona orders his eyes not to weep and his heart not to break. The poem ends after these two commands in the imperative, as if it were no longer possible to marshall words into poetic constraints. In the white space following the final line, we realize that the act of writing this poem has—just barely—averted the persona's collapse, but we can also discern in the emptiness that the grief and anger emblazoned here will recur. Lachner makes it all audible in his setting of stanza 3: the attempt to stave off an encroaching frenzy of despair, the mastery of the moment by means of music (it takes over from words), and the threat of recurrence. This final section of the song begins with a formal convention emblematic of artistic control: the return of the music from the beginning, as if this were to be an A B A three-part form of a sort familiar from thousands of arias and songs. Having admitted the incontrovertible truth, the persona returns to the music that was emblematic of departure, as if to resume his obsessive counting and the voyage into a new land—as much a bleak mental territory as a geographical region. (For Heine, it would become both). But with the invocation of "Mein krankes Herz", the floodgates burst open after a mere eight bars of the music for stanza 1, and any semblance of tidy three-part form is blasted out of the water. With irony aforethought, or so I would like to think, a musical homecoming is derailed. The departure from the previous music (which is, one recalls, *about* departure) begins with the persona once again repeating himself, and this time, he audibly demonstrates that of which he sings. "My sick heart, my sick heart", he declares to music that mirrors rising hysteria to a nicety, every detail evocative of mental extremity. It was a brilliant stroke on Lachner's part to reiterate the phrase exactly and without a break or breath (except the most minimal, snatched on the run) between the two statements in bb. 74–77. The way Lachner shapes the words "krankes Herze" in the vocal line is ineluctably "sick"; for each syllable of "krankes", the slurred intervallic figure rises, such that the higher pitch is on the weaker beat. For the second, ordinarily weaker syllable of the adjective, the singer leaps up a major sixth: the counting figuration from the piano accompaniment has now invaded the vocal line. The slurred appoggiatura on the first syllable of "*Her*– [ze]" resolves downward, not upward, and the aspirate –"h" only accentuates the impression of someone bursting into tears. The entire four bars seem like a musical simulacrum of sobbing, with correct prosody replaced by what one might call psychological prosody, deliberately distorted. As a rendition in music of subjectivity undergoing massive trauma and being almost undone by it on the spot, this song has few peers, in its own time or any other (Ex. 5).

   Rising chromaticism had become a cliché for "Schauer"-effects long before Schubert came along, but what he did with it, as with so much else, became a model for others to challenge or invoke in homage or both. In particular, Schubert's 1817 setting of Schiller's *Gruppe aus dem Tartarus* is a ne plus ultra specimen of this hoary horror symbol, a song in which terror and immensity fuse. Was it perhaps here that Lachner derived the peculiar suitability of ascending chromaticism to denote journeys to dreadful destinations, whether Hades, exile or the awful truth? In the introduction to Schubert's song, we hear chromaticism within chromaticism

Example 5. Franz Lachner. "Wasserfahrt", mm. 64–77, from Sängerfahrt, Op. 33. Vienna, Tobias Haslinger.

before the singer enjoins us to "Listen!": a rising chromatic figure is reiterated sequentially along a larger rising chromatic trajectory. The nesting seems a marvellous structural analogy to the poet's images of water forced through hollow rocks, and souls in dread forced through the passageway to Eternity. The hailstorm of linear chromaticism throws open the all-important question of the goal: where are we going, this music asks? To what terrible destination? By the end, having twisted and turned and traversed virtually every tonal alley possible, the group of souls is back at its starting point. They were in Hades all along, and now they know it. In *Wasserfahrt*, a much shorter chromatic passage imbues the persona's desperate self-injunction with maximal tension. Melody is no longer possible; the driven intensity of the plea is best served by the insistence on one pitch, the verb "Brich" breaking into the bar after the downbeat with palpable urgency. The rising chro-

matic bass is harmonized as a series of parallel first inversion triads, including both E minor and E major harmonies: no root
position terra firma here. In a tiny instance of tragic irony, the
word of negation, "nicht", sounds in major mode, followed swiftly
by the Neapolitan sixth chord, its clash against the reiterated E's
in the vocal line worthy of Schubert himself. This is the sound of
someone on the brink of imminent destruction from within.

In the universe of this song, there is a tailor-made law of repetition: Lachner's persona can only believe the terrible things he says
if he repeats them. At each invocation, the last words of the poem
are set as an authentic cadence, its strength a match for the imperative mode (Ex. 6). "This you *must* do", the persona commands,
but pain immediately impels "Untergang". The plunge downward
of parallel first inversion chords, the directional obverse of the
ascending harmonies only a few bars earlier, has something vertig-
inous about it, brief as it is on first statement. The decrescendo at
this point (bb. 84–85) — pianists, take note — is significant: these
are the dynamics of truth-telling in *Wasserfahrt*, of necessary disil-
lusionment. In order to survive, the persona will have to leave the
treble register of a fantasy he now knows is false and descend to
lower realms of what is real. But because the wish was so precious,
he cannot abandon it summarily and instead arrests the slide
downwards at the precise point where the first injunction, "Brich
mir nicht", began. Before he can descend farther, both into real-
ism and into misery, the Lear-like howl on the oceanic heath must
be repeated and made more frenetic in every way. The texture in
the left hand thickens, the dissonance is intensified by converting
the former first inversion triads into seventh chords, and the point
of greatest emphasis in the naming of "allzugrossen Weh" is unfor-
gettably altered. The adjective is of more import than the noun in
both instances; the existence of sorrow, we know full well by now,
but that it is all too great is the final point of the poem, the spear
that can stab and kill. The first time, Lachner emphasizes the initial syllable, "*all*–zugrossen", on high G, but now at the end, the
first three syllables are all massively underscored, especially " – *gros*
– [sen]". With each musical stanza, the pitch ceiling rises, from F-
sharp in stanza 1, to G in stanza 2, and now — the climax of the
song — high A in stanza 3. As in the setting of the sick heart, the

Example 6. Franz Lachner. "Wasserfahrt", mm. 78–102, from Sängerfahrt, Op. 33. Vienna, Tobias Haslinger.

syncopated rise to the highest pitch in the vocal line against the backdrop of the pounding crotchet tactus in the left-hand part speaks volumes about the anger driving this sustained outcry. Hearing this, no one could mistake how very great this grief is.

The postlude continues and completes the story of this composer's extraordinary musical reading of this poem. Again, the word "Weh" precipitates "steep-down gulfs of liquid fire", a parallel motion descent into the depths. This time, the flight from the realm of illusion plunges lower still, almost but not quite below the bounds of treble register altogether, and the fact that the right hand does not depart the treble clef entirely is significant. Because the fall from the Ideal to the Real goes through natural minor mode (demonstration of the D-natural D-sharp dichotomy in this song and more pianistic, especially at this pace), Lachner must reinstate the leading tone D-sharp at the end, and he does so in a very unorthodox way. One could hardly end *this* song with a textbook cadence. Twice, Lachner bids the right hand rise above E, as if in an attempt to reverse the downward trajectory, but can only go as far as G-natural, the third degree in minor mode. The fantasy-Fatherland in E major is once again negated repeatedly at the end, although it is painfully appropriate that the vision in major mode is situated at the heart of the song, its centre, its interior core. That the halt to the slide downward should be accompanied by grinding dissonance rather than a conventional authentic cadence or plagal cadence is part of what makes the "ending" sound so eerily un-final. The reiterated tonic chords at the close seem a doom-laden tocsin or pulse hinting that the fury and despair brought to sounding life here will recur, and in the fermata-sustained silence at the end of the last measure, we wait for its resumption. The persona may have staved off breakdown by the manufacture of a song, but one does not put an end to misery this profound, a dilemma this terrible, by singing of it only once.

It is easy to see that *Wasserfahrt* is akin to the Schubertian *Lied* in its psychological acuity, its musical revelation of a profound understanding of human nature, its invocation of traditional song form in order suddenly to overthrow it, its challenges for the performers, its abjuration of conventional *Lied* loveliness, its unification of a long song by means of motivic figuration in the piano, and its demonstration of a rare comprehension of Heine's multiple complexities. And yet, *Wasserfahrt* is not some mere clone of Schubert but has its own imprimatur. In particular, I know nothing in Schubert quite like Lachner's notational ploys in this song. By the end, those who see the score understand another horrifying truth Lachner which brings to light in this fashion. Not only does he thereby create a visual analogy for the discrepancy between clock time/calendar time/notated time and one's emotional experience of time, but his persona cannot, this notation tells us, slow down the forces that are now rapidly separating him from something so precious as artistic acceptance in one's own native country. Claustrophobic obsession, panic, near-breakdown: this is no parlour ditty (except in very advanced households) but a work that explores subjectivity brought to the brink of dissolution by rejection issuing from the arbiters of those same cultural traditions in which the persona was raised. For this achievement alone, Lachner deserves a place on the podium with those early nineteenth-century architects of sound who sought to extend the limits of the *Lied.* And it is a lovely thought that Schubert taught other songsters before his premature death, and that they learned so well, both how to be like him and how to be themselves.

CHOPIN AND THE TRADITIONS OF PEDAGOGY

Jim Samson

I should begin by saying that it is impossible to research Chopin's musical education in the way that Larry Todd did Mendelssohn's.[1] In his introduction, Todd cited pedagogical research on Handel, Haydn, Mozart and Beethoven. He went on to speak of the dearth of comparable information on nineteenth-century masters. "We know little", says Todd, "about Schumann's work with Heinrich Dorn in Leipzig, Berlioz's or Liszt's study with Reicha in Paris, Chopin's lessons with Elsner in Warsaw, or Brahms's student days in Hamburg". Naturally, I want to pick up on the Chopin reference there; but not in order to refute Todd's conclusions. He was quite right to suggest that we know little in detail of Elsner's tutelage of Chopin. Nevertheless, I will try, in the second half of this paper, to report what we do know about Chopin's musical education, and what we might infer. In a sense, the spotlight will fall on Józef Elsner, who remains a rather shadowy figure in music history, rather than — or at least as much as — on Chopin himself.

Before tackling that, I should take up an invitation which I think is implicit in Todd's remark, and that is to reflect rather more generally on nineteenth-century pedagogy. It is perhaps not surprising that this subject has received relatively little attention. A canonic view of music history tends to demote pedagogy, since it fosters the notion that genius is set apart and will somehow find its own path. Music sociologists suggest otherwise, and so too do psychologists working in the area of prodigious talent.[2] But even without their help we might, I think, concede that, at the very least, pedagogy can narrow the range of possible paths; it can construct, in other words, some sort of determinate framework for

1. See Larry Todd, *Mendelssohn's Musical Education*, Cambridge 1983. This presents a critical edition of surviving composition exercises. No such primary documentation exists for Chopin.
2. See, for example, Tia DeNora, *Beethoven and the Construction of Genius: Musical Politics in Vienna, 1792–1803*, Berkeley, Los Angeles & London, 1995; also M.J.A. Howe, *The Origins of Exceptional Abilities*, Oxford, 1990.

style formation. And if that is so, its role in the compositional history of music is clearly an important one.

It is when we come to consider in greater detail just how pedagogy might mediate between theory and composition that the difficulties begin, and perhaps especially so for early nineteenth-century music. We may know which theoretical texts were used in a given case, but it is another matter to establish just how they were used, and yet another to say how their use fed into creative praxes. There were strident polemics in music theory at the turn of the eighteenth and nineteenth centuries. But we may well ask how far composers were engaged by them. Or even how far they were capable of registering and evaluating the full significance of competing theories, at least while still in their formative years. The great French *philosophe*, d'Alembert, was distinctly pessimistic. "We all know", he said, "that musicians read nothing, and that they do not even know how to read, but I dare to think that if they were to read anything they would have to read, and even to study, that book".[3] The book in question, incidentally, was Rousseau's Dictionary, and I will return to it very briefly towards the end of the paper. (One is reminded here of Boethius's comments on performing musicians slaving, almost literally, at an art of whose rational basis they have little or no understanding.)

A further difficulty arises from the peculiarly transitional nature of pedagogy during the early nineteenth century. We can relate this in part to wider changes in intellectual and social history, and I will say just a little about each. As to intellectual history, I am certainly not the first to point out that music theory made itself increasingly available to pedagogy during the eighteenth century as it responded to what might be rather crudely described as a shift from doctrinal to rational knowledge. One effect of this shift in intellectual history was to change the status of the musical work to that of a retrospective object and then to locate order and beauty in the work, rather than in what were previously thought to be generalised properties of music.[4] I mean here that we move from a position where theory

---

3. Quoted in Thomas Webb Hunt, *The Dictionnaire de Musique of Jean-Jacques Rousseau*, Diss., North Texas State University, 1967, p. 117.

4 For a full discussion, see James Garnett, *Complexity in Music: A Study in Analytical Thought*, Diss. U. of Oxford, 1992.

constructs an intellectual model of the nature of music, which is essentially prospective, even prescriptive, to one in which theory is derived inductively from actual musical works. This reorientation (which prepared the ground for modern analytic thought) brought some areas of speculative theory within the orbits both of contemporary compositional practice and of pedagogy, culminating in the so-called "practical schools of composition".

As to social history, I refer here to the institutionalisation of music education, and, above all, to the rise of the conservatories, with Paris as principal model. The intensive debates over teaching methods at the Paris Conservatoire, culminating in the conference of 1802, were driven as much by pragmatism as by their ostensible ideology of progress. The real need was to devise teaching methods which might cope efficiently with large numbers of potential teachers and performers—all of which has a familiar ring today, at least in British education. Catel's treatise, triumphant in 1802, took its stand on pragmatism, and this pragmatism invaded all aspects of pedagogy. The counterpart of the instrumental tutor, ubiquitous in the early nineteenth century, was a new kind of dedicated harmony textbook, a textbook in the modern sense.

This transitional status of pedagogy undoubtedly had an important bearing on early nineteenth-century stylistic history. But care is needed in picking our way through this. Above all, we should be cautious about equating the transition from craft instruction to classroom and textbook with the pedagogical divide described by some influential Schenkerians of the generation and circle of Oswald Jonas.[5] The divide in question—separating Fux and thoroughbass from Rameauvian harmonic theories—is, at best, an over-simplification. And it seems clear that, even within Viennese theory, the reality was a good deal more complex than this putative divide suggests, as Ernst Tittel and Robert Wason implicitly demonstrate.[6] If we really are to locate such a divide, it would

---

5. See in particular Oswald Jonas, *Das Wesen des musikalischen Kunstwerks: eine Einführung in die Lehre Heinrich Schenkers*, Vienna, 1934.
6. Ernst Tittel, "Wiener Musiktheorie von Fux bis Schönberg", in: Martin Vogel (ed.), *Beiträge zur Musiktheorie des 19. Jahrhundert*, Regensburg 1966; Robert W. Wason, *Viennese Harmonic Theory from Albrechtsberger to Schenker and Schoenberg*, Ann Arbor, 1982.

probably come rather later with the reification of pedagogical theory which we associate especially with Sechter's method in the 1850s.

There was in any case pedagogy beyond Vienna. Paris had its own very different and highly polemicized divides, closely described by Renata Groth and Cynthia Gessele[7]—most notably between the Rameauvian harmonic theory promoted by the Reys and the Catel system; the Reicha-Cherubini arguments are a rather different matter. We might recall, incidentally, that it was Reicha who taught counterpoint (though not composition) to Liszt and Berlioz, and that Chopin looked in that direction too when he first arrived in Paris. Then there was Berlin—not so much old-fashioned as synthetic, drawing together Rameauvian theories—or versions of them—with something of a living Bach tradition.[8] Bach, of course, needed no rediscovery in 1830, though he was in a sense reinvented. In any case, it was that synthesis—one which assumed a separation, though also an interdependence, of contemporary practice and traditional theory—that informed Mendelssohn's tuition, as Larry Todd pointed out. And I suggest that it was a similar synthesis that shaped the young Chopin, as teaching methods, and specific theoretical texts, made their way from Lwów to Warsaw.

In the late eighteenth century, Lwów was an important centre in Austrian Galicia, very much within the orbit of German culture and ideas. It was almost certainly there, rather than in Vienna itself, that Józef Elsner, a Silesian of German parentage, became acquainted with theoretical texts which were at that time largely unknown in Warsaw. When he moved to Warsaw in 1799, he introduced such texts to the curricula of a complicated succession of teaching institutions: the School of Drama (an offshoot of the National Theatre); the School of Music and Drama (with its

---

7. See Renata Groth, *Die französische Kompositionslehre des 19. Jahrhunderts*, Wiesbaden 1983, and Cynthia Gessele, "B*ase d'harmonie*: A Scene from Eighteenth-Century French Music Theory", in: *Journal of the Royal Musical Association*, Vol. 119 Part 1 (1994), pp. 60–90.

8. See the introduction to Larry Todd, *Mendelssohn's Musical Education*, Cambridge 1983.

Elementary Music School); the Institute of Music and Declamation, or Conservatory; and the High School of Music (which bridged Conservatory and University). There is in fact a confused but interesting institutional history in all this—interesting above all because it rehearsed a struggle for the dignity of musical scholarship which would later be played out on more familiar European stages.

Elsner wrote some of his own teaching materials, including a thoroughbass treatise, a textbook for the Elementary Music School and an influential study of words and music, specifically dealing with the Polish vernacular.[9] There was also a planned Dictionary, rather novel in concept.[10] He further approved a harmony treatise written in Polish and German by Karol Antoni Simon and published in Poznań and Berlin in 1823.[11] This was Chopin's first theory book, and for that reason it merits at least a brief mention. It was one of those modern textbooks I mentioned earlier—of a type that proliferated in the 1820s—and the author spelt out in his preface that it was "designed for amateurs wanting knowledge of the basics in a clear and simple form". What you will not find are lengthy discussions of string division or the sonorous body. The emphasis is strictly on classification and exemplification —of scales, intonations, intervals and their inversions, part movement and chords, with the classifications close to Kirnberger's formulation. The book ends with rudimentary instruction on accompaniment, in the eighteenth- rather than the nineteenth-century sense of that term.

Chopin was given it, presumably by Elsner, in 1823, just after its publication and three years before he entered the High School of Music. It is sometimes supposed that he had private lessons with Elsner at this time, and there is circumstantial, but (as far as I am aware) no documentary, evidence that this was the case. The fact is that, although we know a good deal about Chopin's general education at the Warsaw Lyceum, we know very little of his musical

---

9. *Rozprawa o metrycznosci i rytmicznosci języka polskiego*, Warsaw, 1918.
10. See Alicia Nowak-Romanowicz, *Józef Elsner*, Kraków, 1957, pp. 187–8.
11. Karol Antoni Simon, *Nauka harmonii*, Poznań, 1823. A copy of this can be consulted in the National Library, Warsaw.

training before he entered the High School in 1826, aged sixteen. Even the youthful lessons with the Czech musician Adalbert Żywny remain something of a mystery. The received wisdom about them, trotted out in every monograph, is based on unreliable and contradictory sources dating mainly from half a century after the event. As for the Simon textbook—this would have given Chopin little beyond basic rudiments, but it should be noted that they were rudiments firmly grounded in eighteenth-century traditions.

When we come to his lessons at the High School (often wrongly described as the Conservatory), much more can be said. Programmes and even detailed timetables were announced in the press, along with those for the University, of which Elsner was Professor of Counterpoint and Composition. There are also copious writings by Elsner himself (especially his *Sumariusz*),[12] surviving High School reports and later memoirs by students. More recent secondary sources include institutional histories of both the Conservatory and the University.[13] So what do we know? We know that Chopin had classes with Elsner at the University in Theory, Thoroughbass and Composition. We know the approved texts for the theory and thoroughbass teaching, and we know the broad structure of the composition course. So although there are no extant theory and composition exercises by Chopin, there is a certain amount we can piece together about his musical training. I want to suggest several levels, then, on which his three years at the High School may have shaped his development as a composer.

First, the structure of the composition course had some bearing on his choice of genres in these formative years. Elsner liked to start his pupils off with polonaises, and then to move through independent rondos and variation sets to sonatas, which they would usually begin at the end of the first year. In the second year the generic range was expanded to include orchestral and vocal

12. Jósef Elsner, *Sumariusz moich utworów muzycznych,* ed. Alina Nowak-Romanowicz, Kraków, 1957; original German edn. 1855.
13. See Józef Bielinski, *Królewski Uniwersytet Warszawski (1816–30),* 3 vols., Warsaw, 1907–12, and Stefan Sledzinski (ed.), *150 lat Panstwowej Wyzszej Szkoly muzycznej w Warszawie,* Kraków, *1960.*

textures, while in the third year students were given greater freedom to follow their own inclinations. All this is reflected rather clearly in Chopin's output during the High School years. Two details about the orchestral works are worth a mention, by the way. The choice of *Là ci darem* for Op. 2 might well have been influenced by Elsner, since it was habitually used by him as a model for discussing classical period structures; and there is some concrete, albeit fairly trivial, documentary evidence of help Elsner gave Chopin with the scoring of the *Krakowiak-Rondo*.[14]

A second level of influence concerns more specific compositional practices promoted by Elsner and adopted by several of his students, including Chopin. This is the level, incidentally, on which Michael Heinemann investigated Liszt's response to Reicha's teaching in a useful study.[15] In Chopin's case, it amounts to the generic model for the dance rondos, Op. 5 à la mazur and Op. 14 à la krakowiak; the sequence of the *Schweizerbub* variations; the monothematicism of the Op. 4 Sonata, and details in the construction of themes in that work and elsewhere. All this has been noted by Alicia Nowak-Romanowicz and by Igor Belza.[16] But the most important and durable of these specific practices, in my view, concerns Elsner's approach to the reprise of sonata-form movements, where we can find an intriguing context for some of the formal oddities in Chopin's own early extended works (it is very likely that Elsner may have derived some of these ideas from his knowledge of Reicha's formal theories). We should, by the way, discount Charles Rosen's unfortunate remarks on this subject in *Sonata Forms*.[17] I am thinking especially of the mirror reprise, one of the most characteristic features of Elsner's own music and one that crops up time and again in the music of his students, notably

---

14. See folio 38 of the autograph housed with the Czartoryski Collection of the National Museum in Kraków.

15. Michael Heinemann, "Liszts Fugen und Rejcha", in: *Musiktheorie*, 8 Jahrgang (1993), Heft 3, pp. 14–23.

16. Alicia Nowak-Romanowicz, *Józef Elsner*, and Igor Belza, "Szkoła Elsnera i jej rola w ksztaltowaniu polskiej kultury muzyczny", in his *Portrety romantyków*, Warsaw, 1974, pp. 13-34.

17. "They evidently did not have very clear ideas about sonatas out there in Warsaw", in his *Sonata Forms*, New York and London, 1980, p. 319.

in Nowakowski and Dobrzyński. In due course Chopin carried this Elsner fingerprint through into his mature music, where it changed in radical ways the function of the reprise, and therefore the underlying shape or "plot", to coin a term, of sonata-influenced works.

Third—and most important—we come to Elsner's basic teaching methods, the texts he himself admired and those he used in teaching. The two indispensable theoretical texts were Albrechtsberger, *Anweisung der Composition* and Kirnberger, *Die Kunst des reinen Satzes*.[18] The use of Albrechtsberger suggests, of course, that the harmonically reinterpreted species formed the core of counterpoint teaching at the High School. And that is confirmed by Elsner's avowed practice, common enough among pedagogues, of making his own adaptations of Fux. It is important to emphasize, by the way, that we are speaking of the Albrechstberger treatise of 1790 and not the later hugely popular Seyfried compendium, which prefaced the manual with harmonic theory of rather different, more modern, orientation. But for what it is worth, I may mention that rather later—in the mid-1830s—Chopin was a subscriber to the French translation of that Seyfried compendium.

We know that Elsner had special admiration for the Kirnberger manual from correspondence dating back to his days in Lwów.[19] It was a basic text for Chopin's tuition, as for Mendelssohn's, and it would have given a complementary slant to his counterpoint studies, taking the four-part chorale texture as an harmonic starting point for contrapuntal activation. Happily, I think, music theory has now outgrown a once prevalent tendency to treat late eighteenth-century treatises as pre-histories of tenaciously held present-day positions.[20] It is enough to remark that while much of Kirnberger's theory does indeed resonate in the music of Chopin, it would be rash to speak of primary causes here.

---

18. See Alicia Nowak-Romanowicz, *Józef Elsner*, for a discussion of Elsner's teaching materials and practices.
19. Ibid., p. 187.
20. The point is well and often made in Joel Lester, *Compositional Theory in the Eighteenth Century*, Cambridge, Mass. and London, 1992.

The truth is that theory teaching at Warsaw would have been anything but dogmatic. Judging from the texts and from Elsner's writings, it would have embraced thoroughbass, modified species counterpoint, and chordal progression by *Grundbass*, as practised in Kirnberger. The really key point is that for Chopin, as for Mendelssohn, technical training was firmly rooted in late-eighteenth-century theory, and that for all the polemics, late eighteenth-century theorists were agreed on certain essentials. That point was already made (in just those terms) in the early nineteenth century, and it has been particularly well made by Joel Lester, with the clear implication that some favoured interpretations of the recent past are ripe for revision, and even reversal.[21]

I think the map changes somewhat, incidentally, when we come to consider the training of Liszt and Berlioz. And although I am not really in a position to develop this fully, I suspect that those changes worked their way through into important later differences of style and aesthetic. There are large issues to address here. It is obvious that on one level, Chopin and Mendelssohn drew very different conclusions from a common pedagogical background. But on another level, it was precisely that common background which set them both apart from their contemporaries: this is not just a matter of what was taught, but of attitudes to what was taught; and that incidentally opens up another rather interesting byway which must remain unexplored in this paper.

I cannot really leave this subject without referring to the Delacroix diary entry, reporting Chopin's description of counterpoint, specifically fugue, as "pure logic in music".[22] This belief in the primacy of counterpoint was also affirmed by Elsner in *Sumariusz*. But the source of Chopin's remark was more likely to have been Cherubini, whose treatise he studied in 1841, than anything learnt from his old teacher. Chopin's language is indeed almost identical to Cherubini's. The more interesting part of the entry is, in any case, Chopin's next remark. "The custom", he apparently said, "is to learn the harmonies before coming to the

---

21. Ibid.
22. *The Journal of Eugène Delacroix*, ed. Andre Joubin, New York, 1948, pp. 194–5.

counterpoint". There may have been an implied criticism of contemporary pedagogy here, as some have suggested. But while it is certainly true that Albrechtsberger-Seyfried, to whose French edition Chopin subscribed in the mid 1830s, starts with harmony before coming to counterpoint, so did Kirnberger.

I want to turn now to Elsner's more general thinking about music. One of the clearest presentations of this can be found in the extended preface to his thoroughbass treatise of 1807. Now this preface was actually based very closely—indeed at times almost word for word —on a much more famous text, Forkel's *Allgemeine Geschichte der Musik* of 1788.[23] Elsner almost certainly used the Forkel in teaching, since he took the trouble to have parts of it translated into Polish by his University colleague, the poet Kazimierz Brodziński, of whom more later. In his introduction, Forkel rehearses a well-worn argument about priority, one which concerns aesthetics as much as theory. This is the argument that reached its climax in the Rameau-Rousseau polemic—about the rival claims of voice and instrument, words and music, melody and harmony; and it is a polemic whose resonance reaches right through to more recent discussions of the work concept by Lydia Goehr and Reinhard Strohm. Forkel considers the elements in turn, debates their competing claims and opts in the end for harmony as primary and originating, with melody secondary and derived. Elsner repeats this in his preface, and he also follows Forkel in his location of rhythm and form. Similarly, Forkel makes very plain his allegiance to rhetoric and verbal language as explanatory models for music, referring extensively to Matheson, and he ties this in with a list of genres and affections. Elsner repeats all this too in his preface, and it is worth noting that rhetoric was actually one of the three subtitles of his Composition course at the High School.

This orientation would have been confirmed, moreover, by the other German text Elsner admired, Marpurg's *Kritische Briefe* dating from 1759–64.[24] Alongside lengthy expositions of theory (including early rounds of the disputes with Kirnberger), Marpurg's weekly letters

---

23. See Alicia Nowak-Romanowicz, *Józef Elsner*, pp. 186–7.
24. Ibid., p. 188, note 393.

frequently debated wider aesthetic issues. In one letter, for instance, he expounded Mathesonian rhetoric, while in another he offered concrete proposals as to how the affections should be taught. What this points to is that Chopin was as firmly rooted in eighteenth-century aesthetics as in eighteenth-century theory. Indeed his own, admittedly exiguous, writings on such matters endorse Elsner's essentially eighteenth-century view of music as language. The resonance of this in his later music remains largely unexplored. I have in mind here that there is as much explanatory value in examining his music in terms of genres, figures and tonal types as there is in terms of fundamental structures.

It would be wrong to suggest that Elsner was unresponsive to what we might call modern thought in the early nineteenth century. I pass over his association with Hoffmann and highlight instead certain French and Polish writings he admired greatly, writings which would have pointed his students beyond a Classical aesthetic. One was Rousseau's Dictionary, the book to which d'Alembert referred in that earlier quotation. It would have been the aesthetic, rather than the technical entries, which interested Elsner here, as they did his mentor Forkel in an extended review of the Dictionary. I mean, among others, the entries on genius, on the pathetic, on expression and especially on imitation, where Rousseau took a step beyond an affective towards an expressive aesthetic, celebrating the elusive, suggestive powers of music in ways which depart significantly from classical thought. It goes without saying that any contact Chopin had with Rousseau's ideas on music, *via* his father as well as Elsner, would have been reinforced later in life by his friendship with George Sand. Indeed Rousseau's language in the entry on imitation is echoed quite specifically by Sand in her account of musical meaning in *Impressions et souvenirs*. (I do privately wonder, by the way, if Chopin read Rousseau's resonant entry on *Barcarolles* before writing Op. 60.)

The other French text much beloved of Elsner—he described it as "a beautiful book"—was Grétry's *Mémoirs*,[25] a goldmine of information on music and musical thought in the late eighteenth century. Elsner's sympathy for the book is telling, especially if we

---

25. Grétry, *Mémoires ou Essais sur la musique*, ed. J-H Mees, Brussels/Paris, 1829.

are considering him as a teacher. Grétry's admiration for Rousseau leaps from the pages of the *Mémoirs*, not least in Book 6, much of which is given over to a lengthy discussion of pedagogy. In a nutshell, Grétry takes us a long way from Forkel and Marpurg in his descriptions of just what it takes to be a composer of the first rank. The language here is already that of Romantic idealism — it is sensitivity to poetry, and attunement to the inner truths of the emotions that will lead the aspiring composer to greatness.

Such ideas would have chimed well with Polish writings on the new Romanticism, notably Brodziński's treatise *On Classicism and Romanticism* of 1816. I have already alluded to Elsner's collaboration with Brodziński, who made the translation of Forkel. Among the sections of Forkel translated was that dealing with the rhythmic and melodic characteristics of national musics, including Polish. Elsner actually quoted that passage in one of his own treatises on word setting, and there can be little doubt that such sentiments gave a specifically musical resonance to modern ideas of Romantic nationalism brought to Warsaw from Wilno by, among others, Brodziński himself. (There is another major story here that I will sidestep, about the possible circumbaltic origins of theories of cultural nationalism that reached their most famous exposition in Herder.)

These ideas were commonly discussed in the Warsaw of Chopin's youth. Whether or not the young composer actually attended some of Brodziński's lectures at the University (as he claimed), he would certainly have been familiar with the ideas, especially given the importance attached to them by Elsner. And incidentally, according to the published timetables, Chopin could only have attended those Brodziński lectures if he skipped some of his composition classes with Elsner. There was a timetable clash![26] The appearance in 1829 of Brodzinski's pamphlet *O tańcach*,[27] where he discussed at length the national (lechitic) character of the Poles and, more particularly, the deeper meaning of their national dances, seems especially significant in this connection. It is an early formulation of that equation

---

26. This is pointed out in Tadeusz Frączyk, *Warszawa ml łodości Chopina*, Warsaw 1961.
27. Ibid., pp.182–222.

of folk culture and nationalism which would later (following Herder) prove highly influential, not least in the Slavonic lands, and it is quite possible that it played a part in shaping Chopin's understanding of what he himself called "our national music". The date here is especially crucial. This was precisely the time that he began to compose mazurkas for publication, specified as "not for dancing", and, even more significantly, the time he abandoned the polonaise for several years, probably because it was widely perceived to be a cosmopolitan genre. When he returned to the polonaise he redefined it totally. But that is another essay.

This, then, is the blend of influences which would have acted on the young Chopin through the medium of his teacher Józef Elsner. I suggest that his training at the High School helped create some of the moulds in which his style and aesthetic began to congeal. I suggest further that the late twentieth century has managed both to over-interpret his grounding in eighteenth-century theory, and to neglect altogether his grounding in eighteenth-century aesthetics. It was that dual foundation—technical and aesthetic—that committed Chopin to an essentially Classical view of the musical work, rooted in the immanent, the real, even the rule-bound. In later life I suggest he continued to work more-or-less exclusively on that level, and at a time when a contrary, idealist view of music prevailed. That idealist view was also represented in his Warsaw schooling, but it remained a subordinate presence. And this, I believe, conditioned his later and fuller response to an emergent Romanticism. What Chopin did was to reject in essence an idealist view of the musical work, but to admit compositional criteria derived unmistakably from idealist values, and I include here notions of originality, subjectivity and nationality. One monograph on Chopin described his music as a model, Classically perfect, of the spirit of early Romanticism. I suggest finally that the ingredients of just such a model were all present in his musical education.

PERSONALIA

JOHN NEUBAUER

JOHN NEUBAUER is professor emeritus of Comparative Literature at the University of Amsterdam and a corresponding Fellow of the British Academy (FBA). Before coming to Amsterdam in 1983, Neubauer taught at Princeton University, Case Western University, and the University of Pittsburgh; he was visiting professor at Harvard University, Princeton University and elsewhere. His publications include *Symbolismus und symbolische Logik* (1978), *Novalis* (1980), *The Emancipation of Music from Language* (1986), the *Fin-de-siècle Culture of Adolescence* (1992), and substantial contributions to the Münchner (Hanser) edition of Goethe's works. He is presently editing with Marcel Cornis-Pope a four-volume *History of the Literary Cultures of East-Central Europe*, the first volume of which appeared in May 2004, and includes his article "National Operas in East-Central Europe". His recent publications in the area of word and music also includes "Bartók and the Politics of Folk Music. Musico-Literary Studies in an Age of Cultural Studies" (*Word and Music studies: Defining the Field*. Ed. Walter Bernhart, Steven Paul Scher and Werner Wolf. Amsterdam, 1999. 59–77); "The Return of the Repressed: Language and Music in the Nineteenth Century" (*Anglistentag 1004. Aachen*. Ed. Lilo Moessner and Christa Schmidt. Trier, 2005. 199–209); and "Hoffmanns vertellingen en andere verhalen over instrumentale muziek" (*Welke taal spreekt de muziek? Muziekfilosofische beschouwingen*. Ed. Erik Heijerman and Albert van der Schoot. Budel, 2005. 23–37).

JANET SCHMALFELDT

JANET SCHMALFELDT is Associate Professor of Music Theory at Tufts University. She is the author of Berg's *"Wozzeck": Harmonic Language and Dramatic Design* and has published articles on the relation of analysis to performance, on Berg's Piano Sonata Op. 1, on aspects of cadence, form, and voice leading in eighteenth- and nineteenth-century music, and on an ideology that she has identified as the "Beethoven-Hegelian tradition." Her forthcoming book develops philosophical and analytic perspectives on musical form as process in early nineteenth-century European music. She was elected Vice-President of the Society for Music

Theory (SMT) in 1995; in 1999, she completed a two-year term as SMT President. She was honoured to present a keynote address to the Society for Music Theory in 2003 and to the Dutch-Flemish Society for Music Theory in 2004. In the spring of 2005, she participated in an international workshop in Freiburg, Germany, on communicative strategies in late eighteenth-century music. Subsequent presentations have addressed works of Mendelssohn in Tallinn and aspects of Chopin's music in Freiburg and Warsaw. Her performances in the role of pianist have included solo, concerto, and chamber music.

SCOTT BURNHAM

SCOTT BURNHAM is Professor of Music at Princeton University, where he served as Chair of the Music Department from 2000to 2008.He is the author of *Beethoven Hero* (Princeton, 1995), translator of A. B. Marx, *Musical Form in the Age of Beethoven* (Cambridge, 1997), and co-editor of *Beethoven and His World* (Princeton, 2000). Forthcoming writings include "Late Styles," in *Rethinking Schumann* (Oxford University Press), and a chapter on Hugo Riemann and Beethoven's Op. 31 piano sonatas, for *Riemann Perspectives* (Cambridge University Press).

SUSAN YOUENS

SUSAN YOUENS is the J. W. Van Gorkom Professor of Music at the University of Notre Dame. She has published numerous scholarly articles on the 19th-century Lied and eight books on the songs of Schubert, Schumann, Wolf, and others, including Heinrich Heine and the Lied (Cambridge, 2007), Schubert's Late Lieder: *Beyond the Song Cycles* (Cambridge, 2002), *Schubert, Müller, and Die schöne Müllerin* (Cambridge, 1997), *Schubert's poets and the making of lieder* (Cambridge, 1999), *Retracing a Winter's Journey: Schubert's Winterreise* (Cornell, 1991), *The Mörike Lieder of Hugo Wolf* (Cambridge, 2000), and *Franz Schubert: Die schöne Müllerin* (Cambridge, 1992). She is currently working on two books, one entitled *Schumann in the World* and the other *A Social History of the Lied.*

JIM SAMSON

JIM SAMSON is Professor of Music at Royal Holloway, University of London, and Professor II at the Norwegian University of Science and Technology. He has published widely (including seven single-authored books, and seven edited or co-edited books) on the music of Chopin and on analytical and aesthetic topics in nineteenth- and twentieth-century music. He is one of three Series Editors of *The Complete Chopin: A New Critical Edition* (Peters Edition, in progress). In 1989 he was awarded the Order of Merit from the Polish Ministry of Culture for his contribution to Chopin scholarship, and in 2000 he was elected a Fellow of the British Academy. Among his recent publications are *The Cambridge History of Nineteenth-Century Music* (Cambridge, 2002), *Virtuosity and the Musical Work: The Transcendental Studies of Liszt* (Cambridge, 2003), which was awarded the Royal Philharmonic Book Prize in 2004, and (with J. P. E. Harper-Scott) *An Introduction to Music Studies* (Cambridge, 2009). He is currently working on a book entitled *Betwixt and Between: Music in the Balkans.*

DARLA CRISPIN

Dr. DARLA CRISPIN is Senior Research Fellow in Creative Practice of the team of Research Fellows within the Orpheus Research Centre in Music (ORCiM) and at the Royal College of Music. Her research concentrates upon performance and philosophy in musical modernism and post-modernism, with particular emphasis on the Second Viennese School.

EDITORS
Darla Crispin
Kathleen Snyers

SERIES EDITOR
Peter Dejans

AUTHORS
John Neubauer
Janet Schmalfeldt
Scott Burnham
Susan Youens
Jim Samson

LAY-OUT
Wilfrieda Paessens, Ghent

PRESS
Grafikon, Oostkamp
Bioset, 100gr

ISBN 978 90 5867 7341
D/2009/1869/36
NUR 663

© 2009 by Leuven University Press /
Universitaire Pers Leuven / Presses Universitaires de Louvain
Minderbroedersstraat 4, B–3000 Leuven (Belgium)